KIDDIE ENGLISH

A GUIDE TO TEACHING KINDERGARTEN AND PRIMARY SCHOOL CHILDREN

REVISED EDITION

PROF. VIRGINIA S. B. CALHOUN

UNIVERSIDAD AUTÓNOMA DE CHIAPAS

LANGUAGE SCHOOL

B.A. DEGREE PROGRAM IN

TEACHING ENGLISH AS A FOREIGN LANGUAGE

2011

TABLE OF CONTENTS

INTRODUCTION: TEACHING KIDS

Most English teachers work with children at some point during their teaching careers, due to preference or to necessity. For some teachers, it is a wonderful experience. They enjoy children's spontaneity, playfulness, humor, curiosity, and affectionate natures. Children are often enthusiastic about learning, full of energy, quick to imitate the teacher's pronunciation and proud of their new vocabulary. Some teachers have a natural affinity, understanding and empathy with children, or relate to their students in the same way that they relate to their own sons and daughters.

However, other teachers hate working with children. The didactic techniques that teachers learned in the university don't seem to apply, the children get bored easily and are difficult to control, and testing illiterate kindergarteners seems impossible. While English language teachers are trained to give classes in English from the beginning, using cognates and examples to help students understand, young children often don't have enough vocabulary in their native language or knowledge of the world to recognize those cognates and examples. Teachers may give boring classes in the native language, shout at the children, fail many students or give arbitrary grades, and feel frustrated because students don't learn. If frustrated teachers have to continue working with children because of limited job opportunities, they may hate both their work and their students. Such teachers can see a 30 year professional career in teaching children like a 30 year prison sentence!

This situation is not necessary. Although having a natural affinity with children is an advantage, many of the new teachers' problems working with children can be solved if future English teachers learn appropriate techniques for planning children's classes, relating to children, motivating them, finding appropriate activities for different stages in the child's life, presenting new material in English to children who don't yet understand the language, testing children who can't read or write yet, controlling the group and engaging children's interest.

This manual is designed to help English teachers and students of didactics with these techniques. In addition, there is a section with songs, games, stories and pictures which teachers can incorporate in their lessons or use as rewards. Most of the ideas and all of the drawings come from the author's 20 years of teaching experience or from observing other successful teachers. Many of the songs and games are traditional parts of U.S. or British folk culture from the public domain; a few are original works by the author or the author's adaptations of traditional songs and games. Some articles of further interest easily available by Internet are recommended at the end of each unit. It is the author's hope that this manual will help future generations of EFL teachers to be effective, creative and satisfied in kindergartens and primary schools around the world.

ABOUT THE AUTHOR

Virginia Stuart Blair Calhoun, a native of Wooster, Ohio, U.S.A., received her B.A. in Liberal Arts from Kenyon College in Ohio in 1980 and her ICELT (English language teaching certification) from the British Council in 2006. She has lived in Chiapas, married to Francisco Millán Velasco, since 1982. With over 20 years of English teaching experience, Professor Calhoun has taught at all levels from kindergarten to university. Professor at the Campus III Language School of the Universidad Autónoma de Chiapas since 2000, Virginia Calhoun has taught Teaching Methodology for Kindergarten and Primary School, Introduction to Didactics and other subjects in the B.A. Program there, as well as presenting talks at several national English Language Teaching conferences. Along with her colleagues Maria Luisa Avila Losada and Ivan Perez Roman, Professor Calhoun is also coauthor of *The Long and Winding Road: A life story of the English Language* (UNACH, 2010).

WHEN I WAS A CHILD...

PRESENTATION

Can you remember when you were a child? Look at the picture, read the phrases, then close your eyes and try to remember how it felt to be a child. Do you remember your favorite clothes? A special toy? The things that made you feel good? What did you like best about school? Did you have any teachers that you loved? What did they do? Most children have some negative experiences, too. Were there any children who were cruel to you? Did you ever feel frightened or angry at school? Did you have any teachers who made you feel bad? If you can remember being a child, it will be easier for you to identify with your young students. You were once a little child like them, and one day they will be an adult like you. Children are not an alien species. They are people like you. When you teach children, you can help people who feel the way you did. Did you have a teacher who inspired you? You can be that teacher for the next generation of children.

You have the most exciting job in the world. When you know how to work with children, you will enjoy your teaching career immensely. I dedicate this manual to all the teachers, past, present and future, who genuinely enjoy children and sincerely want to help them. You have inspired and guided me.

Good luck and enjoy your teaching,

Virginia Calhoun

GLOSSARY

Atmosphere: The "feeling" of a classroom (peace, tension, friendliness or aggression) caused by the relationships between teachers and students, and among students.

Christmas carols: Special songs for Christmas time.

Circle games: Simple games that children stand or sit in a circle to play.

Corporal punishment: Hitting or hurting children when they behave badly.

ESA (Engagement, Study, Activation): Technique for capturing students' interest in the material first, then letting students analyze the material, and finally asking students to use the material.

Finger games: Simple games with rhymes: children move their fingers to imitate objects.

Forcible pressure: When an adult physically moves or obligates a child to obey by force.

Isolation: The child cannot participate in classroom activities with his/her classmates.

Pacing: How quickly the teacher changes activities to maintain children's interest.

Peer pressure: The pressure that friends and classmates exercise on each other.

Realia: Real objects (school supplies, clothing, food, etc.) that can be used for teaching.

Stages: Periods in a child's maturation.

UNIT 1: LESSON PLANNING AND CLASSES IN ENGLISH

VOCATION

How much of teaching ability with small children is learned technique and how much is natural aptitude? Much of being a good teacher depends on your vocation: your basic love of teaching, love for kids and love of your subject: English. Your character, including your emotional side, is very important. Just as professional singers must have a natural talent for music or professional football players must have a natural ability for sports, so professional teachers must have a natural enjoyment of students. If you have a natural empathy with children and you genuinely enjoy their company, you will probably be a good teacher with them. If you share common ground with children—you enjoy playing, you like games and songs, you are active and kinesthetic (physical), you have a sense of humor and you are enthusiastic, you can become an excellent teacher.

However, even if you do not have natural empathy with children, you can develop that empathy if you have the motivation to do so. If you want to understand and like kids, if you observe them and practice interacting with them, you can find your vocation as a primary school or kindergarten teacher. Obviously, your training is very important. Training and experience will give you techniques that will improve your teaching, make you more efficient, and give you good practical ideas for your classes. You may be surprised at how your feeling about children changes and becomes more positive with more knowledge about them and more experience.

A GOOD TEACHER IS:	A GOOD TEACHER:
➤ Confident, self-assured	➤ Enjoys kids and empathizes with them
➤ Tolerant of others, not perfectionist	➤ Enjoys playing, comfortable with body.
➤ Patient, relaxed	➤ Has a sense of humor and a sense of fun
➤ Respectful of others	➤ Has passion for teaching, enjoys subject
➤ Professionally ethical, moral	➤ Appreciates and respects others
➤ Affectionate, demonstrative	➤ Works hard, prepares classes

Children can sense when a teacher really appreciates them. They know if you like them, if you enjoy their games, if you can sincerely relate to their jokes and ideas. If you get a job as a primary school or kindergarten teacher, but you feel uncomfortable with children, you will have a terrible time at work every day—unless you learn how to love them. Teachers who cannot relate to children will find the children difficult, the activities ridiculous and embarrassing, and the pay insufficient. If you don't like children, you should either learn to like them, or else go to work at a different job.

To relate well to children, you need to discover your own "inner child," the childlike part of yourself. You need to remember how you felt as a child, what you wanted to do, and accept that part of yourself. It is very hard to love children if you don't love the childlike part of yourself. This childlike part is your spontaneous, emotional side, the part of you that doesn't care what people will say, the part that wants to play and feel and be free. This part of you doesn't worry about doing things correctly or getting it right. It doesn't care about looking ridiculous, acting stupid or singing out of tune. This is your expressive side.

If you appreciate your own childlike qualities, you can appreciate children. The most important asset you have as a teacher is the empathy you have with children.

The ability to understand other people, appreciate them and find something good in them is very important for a teacher. Your job is to work with people, not books or machines. You may use books or machines to help your work, but people, children, are the center of your work. Social skills, natural sympathy for other people, kindness, tolerance, appreciation and a spirit of joy are the basic tools of a teacher. You will have to relate to colleagues, superiors and parents, as well as children.

Teachers who are irritable, perfectionist or overly-critical, indifferent to others, offended by immaturity, humorless, rigid or judgmental will have problems with their students and hate their jobs. If you are generally impatient and intolerant, if you usually criticize others and see only their deficiencies and faults, you will be miserable as a teacher. You will probably feel angry, frustrated and exasperated most of the time. If this is your character, you need to change if you want to be happy as a teacher. Being irritable and intolerant will make your own life miserable, as well as the lives of your students. If you can't be tolerant and you don't want to change, don't work at a job you will hate. Be a translator, a simultaneous interpreter or write bilingual guide books. Don't teach children.

Teaching children is a privilege and a vocation. Teaching is a sacred calling, an opportunity to make an enormous difference to children. You can have an immense influence on their lives and attitudes. You can help their self-esteem and their acceptance of themselves. You can show them interesting and exciting new worlds. You can help them love the English language, love learning, love experimenting courageously with new ideas. You won't earn a lot of money, but you will have a great reward: the love and sincere appreciation of your students.

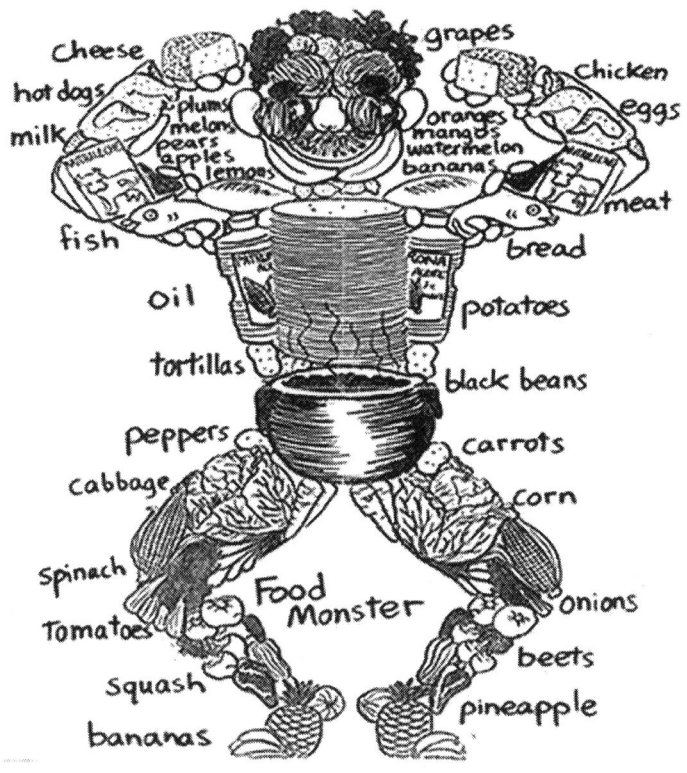

cheese
hot dogs
milk
plums
melon
pears
apples
lemons
oranges
mangos
watermelon
bananas
grapes
chicken
eggs
meat
fish
oil
bread
tortillas
potatoes
peppers
black beans
cabbage
carrots
corn
spinach
Food
Monster
onions
Tomatoes
beets
squash
pineapple
bananas

CLASS PLANNING

The most important skill a new teacher needs to learn is how to plan a class. Most of the problems which teachers face can be solved with good class planning. Good planning gives students motivation, helps them learn effectively, gives the teacher authority and presence, and improves the atmosphere of the class and the students' behavior. Class planning is indispensable for teachers. A carefully planned class is dynamic, fun and effective at helping students learn English.

PLAN YOUR CLASSES THE WAY YOU PLAN A MENU.

Mole is delicious, but can you imagine a dinner with mole chips, followed by mole soup, mole with rice, mole with chicken, mole with beans and mole with bananas for dessert, accompanied by a cold glass of... mole? Just as you like variety in your food, with hot and cold, sweet and salty, rich and light dishes, in the same way students appreciate variety in their classes. Include group work, individual work and pair work, as well as whole class work. Include at least 2 or 3 of the 4 skills in each class. Vary your activities and surprise your students with something new. Alternate activities that use visual abilities with auditory, kinesthetic or analytical activities. Plan a varied and delicious class.

TEACHING METHODS:

TEACHING TECHNIQUES- ENGAGE, STUDY ACTIVATE

When you plan a class, begin by **engaging** your students. Start with an interesting presentation, something that captures their attention. Relate the new material to their lives and their context, use realia, tell a story, sing a song, play a game or show them an interesting picture.

After you have engaged their interest, they are motivated to understand the new material and learn to use it. At this point, they **study** the new material, learning when and how to use it and finding out what it means. You explain the material to them or else give them examples to let them discover it. This is the stage where they learn grammar rules or the meaning of new vocabulary.

Finally, you **activate** the material, giving the students a chance to use it, experiment with it, practice it and apply it in context. The students might write, speak or read a passage that uses the new material. You could give them a song, game, drawing or role play with this new material.

Notice that you give them the same material (vocabulary, structures) in each of the 3 steps, to reinforce their learning. Students do not learn material because the teacher explains it once. They learn because they are engaged and interested in the material, they understand it, and they have a chance to use it in context.

This strategy is called ESA—Engage, Study, Activate, from page 84 of Jeremy Harmer's book, _The Practice of English Language Teaching, 3rd Edition,_ published by Longman in 2001. In one class period, the teacher can present one or many selections of material, both new and reviewed, but for each selection, the teacher will repeat the ESA pattern, engaging the students' attention again about the next selection of material, studying it, and activating it.

THE ABCs OF CLASS PLANNING IN CHILDREN'S EFL CLASSES

A: Age Appropriateness

Plan your class according to the age, preferences, abilities and limitations of your students. Don't give them themes in English that they cannot understand yet in their first language or activities that will seem "babyish" to them. Kindergarteners can't read, first graders don't know how to tell time, second graders don't know much grammar in their first language and sixth graders won't sing infantile songs. Talk with their regular teachers and find out what their capacities and preferences are.

B: Balance

Include a variety of activities: active and quiet; whole class activities with team work, small group work, work in pairs and individual work; teacher-centered or student-centered activities; more controlled or freer activities. You need to include a variety of contrasting elements. Each activity in the class contributes to the balance and the total effect.

C: Cohesion

Classes need to be coherent, congruent and connected. Plan classes with the ESA (Engage/Study/Activate) formula, recycling the same language elements. Repeat this ESA formula 2 or 3 times per class, every time you introduce new information. Children cannot learn everything that the teacher presents with just one activity. Use different activities to teach each topic. Each new activity should reinforce the previous activity, or extend it. For example, teach colors then add vocabulary for clothes, combining clothes with color words. Combine animal vocabulary with "can," "can't" and verbs—"The fish can swim. The fish can't fly." Each activity that the teacher uses should have an objective. Sing "Old MacDonald" to reinforce animal words, emphasize the questions and answers in the conversation between the wolf and the little girl in "Little Red Riding Hood" to teach question words, or play "Stop!" as a repetition drill for verbs. Activities need to be related. Unrelated activities may be fun but don't teach anything.

D: Details

Prepare every detail of your class. Find, invent or adapt stories, songs or games that you can use and memorize them. If you invent songs, specify the tune and make sure your words work with that tune. (For example: "Sing to the tune of the ABC song.") Planning a class with "a story about colors" is insufficient. Write the story, plan who your characters are and what happens to them. If you invent a game, bring all the necessary materials, invent clear rules and give your game a name. Repeat the same activities another day, especially if students like them. Prepare the materials you will need; practice giving the instructions and imagine any possible problems.

E: English

Use a maximum of English in the class. Convey your meaning clearly by non-verbal means as you speak English so your students will understand the language. This is very motivating for students and builds up their confidence. If you revert to their native language every time you want to make things clear, the students will feel that they cannot understand English, or that the native language is the only real means of communication.

F: Fun

Students learn better when they are having fun. Convert drills into songs or games. Use competitive games for routine tasks like checking homework or reviewing. Use humor and exaggeration to make your classes funny and fun.

GIVING CLASSES IN ENGLISH

One of the biggest problems new teachers face is deciding how much English to use in the classroom. Why is it important to use English as the basic language of your English class?

- ➤ To increase listening proficiency and vocabulary.
- ➤ To give a model for speaking, to give basic patterns and structures in English.
- ➤ To help students think in English, using authentic language.
- ➤ To establish the context for new vocabulary, especially for words with multiple meanings.
- ➤ To help students acquire language unconsciously; get a "feel" for English.

➢ To help students understand how English vocabulary and structures are used in real conversation, as well as when and how often they are used.

➢ To help students manage unfamiliar vocabulary, look for gist (basic meaning) and ignore unnecessary words.

➢ To develop students' paralinguistic skills for interpreting language (catching visual or auditory clues).

➢ To increase students' self-confidence and show them that they can understand English.

➢ To show that English is a real means of communication, not just an exercise.

Classes in English will teach students to understand much more language than classes in the children's native language, but the teacher needs to use special techniques to be able to communicate in English.

CAN TEACHERS GIVE BEGINNING CLASSES IN THE TARGET LANGUAGE?

According to some studies, from 60 to 80% of normal communication is non-verbal. Clothes, posture and facial expression, tone of voice and where our bodies and eyes turn: all these things express feelings and give the context to words. When teaching children, we can exaggerate these non-verbal clues, supplementing them with pictures, songs, games, stories, books and mime, to help children understand and enjoy the class **IN ENGLISH.**

Students from the UNACH (Universidad Autónoma de Chiapas) received a class exclusively in an unfamiliar language (German or Tzotzil) to illustrate these techniques. In an oral check after the class, students answered questions correctly about all the unfamiliar vocabulary below. They understood all the language used in the class, and even produced some words in the unknown language ("My name is….," "Yes," "No," the words to the song used in the class and all the words for colors and clothing).

Greetings: Hello. How are you? Fine? Very good. No, Yes. That's good. What's your name? My name is X. Is your name X? Sit down, please. Please stand up.

Game: Stop! Stop! Walk! Dance! Eat! Write! Read! Laugh! Sing! Cry! Count!

Song: Can you <u>sing</u>? No, I cannot. Yes, I can. Can you: walk, dance, eat, write, read, laugh, cry, count?

Game: Touch something red. That is red. That is not blue. Red, Yellow, Green, Blue, White, Black.

Paper Dolls: The shirt, the skirt, the pants, the shoes, the blouse.

Stories:

<u>Cinderella</u> in German: sad, happy, good, bad, beautiful, ugly, sit, dance, dress, shoe.

<u>The Foolish Boy</u> in Tzotzil: read, write, count, sing, dance, laugh, walk, can you, I can't, sad.

Questions: Do you want to play? Do you want to sing?

Methods Used

How can a teacher explain vocabulary and teach in a language that the students don't know? The following methods are helpful for showing beginning students what you mean, even when they don't yet understand the language.

Context clues: Shaking hands with each student as s/he enters the classroom makes them understand that "hello" is a greeting.

Modeling: The teacher says the word "hello" in the target language, with appropriate actions (standing in the doorway as the students enter, smiling, shaking hands) so the students can imitate these words.

Verbal examples: The names the teacher uses to present the language for asking and telling names give the students the clues they need to understand the activity. "My name is Virginia." "What's your name? Is your name Michael Jackson?"

Gestures: The teacher uses standard gestures to indicate meaning: nodding for "yes," shaking head for "no," moving hands palm down for "sit down," or palms up for "stand up," putting finger over mouth for "be quiet."

Mime: In the game "Stop!" the teacher mimes a verb and students naturally imitate teacher and understand the meaning. To show the meaning of "Stop!" the teacher puts hands up, palms out, like a policeman. Students' participation makes the activity more fun and more memorable.

Reception before production: Students hear and understand the verbs in the game "Stop!" but they do not have to pronounce them yet.

Limited responses: Students learn to say "yes" and "no" from teacher's standard gestures of nodding or shaking head. Then they can participate actively, answering "yes" or "No" to teacher's questions, "Is this black/red/blue?" even before they can produce color words. The teacher would introduce more vocabulary in the same way: "Is this red or blue?" "Is this a shirt or a blouse?"

Repetition: In the song "Can you run?" students repeat the same words, only changing the verb in each verse. "The Foolish Boy" story repeats key words.

Songs and Games: Repetition drills in the context of songs or games, as mentioned above, are more fun and more memorable than spoken or written repetition drills. Most songs and games involve repetition and are a natural medium for drills. Like the other activities here, they involve whole language chunks, rather than isolated words.

Realia: Students see and touch real objects that are "red" or "green," beginning with markers, to emphasize that the words refer to colors, and continuing with their own clothing, to make the game more personal.

Movement: Students run and touch "something blue" or "something yellow." They use movements with the "Can You Run?" song. This involves children, who are naturally kinesthetic, and fixes the vocabulary in their minds.

Toys and dolls: Students learn the words "shirt, pants, skirt, blouse" and "shoes" from the paper dolls. These words are combined with the color words already learned. Children love to play with toys, so the lesson is fun.

Stories: People of all ages, but especially children, love stories. Stories give words a context and pre-teach structures.

Familiar material: The story of Cinderella is familiar to the students, so they can understand it with minimal clues. "The Foolish Boy" is a new story, but it contains familiar patterns and a lot of repetition.

Pictures: The teacher can point to pictures in a book, draw or bring photos. In the Cinderella story, the pictures show the students that this is Cinderella. They understand the words "sisters, mice, rat, pumpkin, fairy" and "prince" from the pictures. In "The Foolish Boy," the students understand the meaning from the pictures on the board and the stick puppet of the foolish boy.

Recycling: The song "Can you sing?" recycles verbs from the game "Stop!" The paper dolls and clothing recycles color words from the game "Touch something red." The Cinderella story recycles the word "shoe" from the paper dolls. "The Foolish Boy" recycles verbs from the song and the "Stop!" game.

Facial expression and posture: The teacher uses a sad facial expression and bent over posture (curved spine) to show what "Poor Cinderella!" means. The angry father in "The Foolish Boy" stands with his hands on his hips in an aggressive posture. During the story, the teacher will give the emotional context for the words with his/her face and posture, to make the story more exciting as well as easier to understand.

Vocal expression: This includes pitch, speed and timbre. Like facial expression, vocal expression gives an emotional context to the words, distinguishes the speaking characters in a story and indicates meaning. The wicked stepsisters should sound wicked, with abrasive shouts. The foolish boy sounds enthusiastic—and foolish!

GIVING CLEAR INSTRUCTIONS IN BASIC ENGLISH

Remember that your students may not know any English at all when you first meet them. You need to make your instructions clear in non-verbal ways, while you establish the key words and phrases they will need.

Model the activity as you give instructions, so students can see and hear simultaneously. For desk activities, put a large poster on the board, with the same pictures or task that the students will do. Do the first activity with markers as an example. After that, you can mime the technique (circle, match, write, color, cross out) repeatedly, using the poster.

Use short, simple instructions. Repeat and emphasize the same key words and phrases ("**Open** your **books**. Your **book**." "Good. **Open** it.") all year. Do not vary them.

Students will learn them by repetition and understand them by your modeling. Eliminate extra words. Use the same short orders every day: *"Open your books to page 14, please."*

Use colors, numbers, letters or pictures to simplify the activity. For example: in a Concentration (Memorama) game, use red cards for words, blue cards for pictures. When you give your instructions, say "Turn over a blue card." instead of "Turn over one of the cards with a picture of a verb on it."

Use examples and realia. "Color it red. Red. Like Gaby's sweater." "Write your name. Maria, Daniel, Juan: your name."

Use contrasting words and opposites. "Color it red. Not blue; red." Check comprehension by asking questions with contrasting words. "Do I circle or cross out? Is this red or blue?"

Use familiar words and cognates, especially with older children. For example: use *prohibit* instead of *forbid*. "This is a spider. Like Spiderman."

Use your best students as models. "Yes Alejandro! That's good! See Alejandro's bear? He colored it red." Let your students ask questions, clarify or translate into their native language. Respond to them in English. Your best students can translate for their classmates so that you can speak only English. Accept their use of their native language, but be a model of English for them.

Repeat the instructions with different techniques if the students didn't understand the first time.

NEVER ASK, "DO YOU UNDERSTAND?" STUDENTS WILL ALWAYS SAY, "YES," EVEN WHEN THEY DIDN'T UNDERSTAND ANYTHING. Check comprehension with expressions like "Show me," "Point to" or "Where is?"

CONCLUSION

Well-planned classes in English, with a variety of appropriate activities that recycle new vocabulary and structures, are fun for children and help them learn. Use verbal and non-verbal techniques to communicate with your students in English from the beginning.

EXERCISE:

Identify the problems in the following activities

1. The teacher gives the kindergarten class three games in a row: Duck-Duck-Goose, London Bridge, and Hokey Pokey.

2. The teacher gives instructions for a kindergarten game: "Jump! First move the chairs. I mean, stand up. Now get in a circle. Get the tables out of the way first. Now jump!"

3. The teacher explains the new vocabulary, then asks, "Does everybody understand what 'grass' means? Good."

4. The teacher needs to use the word "sun," but the children, whose native language is Spanish, don't know it. "Sun quiere decir sol," says the teacher.

5. Teacher invents a story about a prince, a fox, a giant, and 3 wishes, to illustrate color vocabulary.

6. Teacher has 3rd graders copy words about feelings (angry, sad, happy, etc.) from the board, together with their translations in their native language.

7. Teacher begins the class asking students to open their books to the explanation of the past simple of "to be" on page 63.

8. Students in 5th grade have trouble remembering the past participles of verbs. Teacher tells students to write the past participles 5 times each.

9. 6th graders don't understand the word "shoulders". When teacher draws shoulders, students confuse "head," "neck" and "shoulders."

10. Teacher teaches names of animals to 2nd graders, using toys. Then students match animal words with verbs for animal's actions, "fly," "swim," "jump," "sing," etc.

11. 1st graders have problems remembering English vowels. They confuse the English "E" with the Spanish "I."

MICROTEACHING 1: ENGAGEMENT/STUDY/ACTIVATION

Plan a 50 minute class for students of your age including 3-6 activities. Organize the activities in the ESA form. Your activities should be varied (quiet-active, group work-pair work-individual work) and fun. Have one extra activity ready in case you finish your material early.

(Please use the blank pages at the end of each unit for your own notes)

UNIT 2: STAGES OF CHILDHOOD DEVELOPMENT: KINDERGARTEN & PRIMARY SCHOOL

INTRODUCTION

Children and adults learn in very different ways. Adults are good at reading and writing, at analyzing grammar and structures, and at sitting quietly in a classroom. Adults often have high motivation to learn English because they need it for their studies, work or travel. They can concentrate for long periods of time and review what they learned by reading their class notes.

Children have different abilities. They can imitate pronunciation very well, they are self-confident, and they are not embarrassed to try speaking in a new language. They participate enthusiastically in fun activities and they have lots of energy. Children usually love their teachers and they will work hard for their teachers' approval. Children can memorize songs and rhymes in English more easily than adults, they are more creative and imaginative, and they often enjoy learning more than adults do.

Teachers need to adapt their classes according to the age and abilities of their students. In order to do this, new teachers need to learn about children's stages of development, the special interests and abilities that children have at each stage, and the limits to their learning.

CHARACTERISTICS OF CHILDREN AT DIFFERENT AGES

KINDERGARTEN STUDENTS

Characteristic: Most kindergarteners are self-confident and kinesthetic. They do not feel embarrassed about performing in front of others. Most kindergarteners love games, singing and drawing. Kindergarteners are good at imitating movements

Strategies: Foment and reinforce their self-confidence so they can learn more easily.

Use mime, sounds, facial and corporal expression and tone of voice to show meaning of words, and ask the students to imitate these techniques. Use songs with movements for repetition drill and pronunciation, to reinforce the meaning of language and develop their "lyrical ear" for English. Use active games that involve movement for repetition drill, to channel energy and to control group. Use drawing to calm students, to test them, as drill to reinforce language, and as a reward.

Characteristic: Kindergarteners are auditory. Kindergarteners can imitate pronunciation very well. They can't analyze or create abstract categories yet. They can't read or write.

Strategies: Use language in context, not isolated words. Give children a good stock of classroom phrases, vocabulary and songs before they learn to read. Don't use written language or homework yet. Try to avoid using the native language, so child becomes accustomed to spoken English, learns to think in English and not translate. Don't compare subtle grammatical differences. Use different grammatical structures in context. Use context, modeling, pictures, mime. Don't give abstract explanations. Control group so students can hear input. There must be constant input of simple, repetitive language.

Characteristic: Small children love familiar stories

Strategies: Use stories to develop children's ear for language. Let students repeat key phrases for pronunciation, vocabulary, word order. Repetitive stories are good. Use them as a reward, and to calm students.

Characteristic Kindergarteners tend to be affectionate.

Strategies: Give students physical affection, positive reinforcement. Learn children's names and use them. Compliment children on their talents, their clothes or toys. Express interest in them. Be sincere—children can sense hypocrisy. If you don't like small children and enjoy working with them, don't teach them. Never abuse them sexually, physically or emotionally.

Characteristic: Because of their limited experience of the world, kindergarteners are often self-centered, inflexible and insensitive.

Strategies: Take into account children's inability to see things from others' perspective. Explain others' feelings. Treat children fairly, explain rules thoroughly, give reasons for exceptions.

Characteristic: Small children have a short attention span. They are easily distracted

Strategies: Pace activities to change every 5-10 minutes. Alternate quiet and active activities, depending on students' moods and needs. Engage attention with whole-group activities, good pacing, ask questions to whole group, then call on specific students.

After Kindergarten, children gradually change and become more like adults.

PRIMARY SCHOOL: Stages In Development And Learning Styles

FIRST GRADE:

Description: Children sit at desks, usually in rows. Games with movement have to be in one place. There is no space inside the classroom for circle games, and active games with a lot of running are more difficult. Children are more sophisticated. They begin to analyze and to recognize symbols, they begin to read in their native language and they can learn the names of letters in English. (They should not begin to read or write in English until 2nd grade.) They can relate a symbolic picture to a concept. Don't teach abstract concepts (grammar, reading a clock, etc.) that students don't yet understand in their native language.

Attention span: 5-10 minutes.

Continue: Songs with movements, familiar stories with lots of repetition, toys, realia, games with mime, finger games, rhymes.

Eliminate: Circle games, "Where is Thumbkin?" song.

Add: Row games (e.g. "Hold up something *red*," "Put your book *under* your desk," "Show me your *ruler*.") The first row in which everyone follows the teacher's instructions gets a point. The first row to get ten points wins.

Team games (See Unit 5)

Desk Activities ("Color the *cat red*," "Circle *run*," "Cross out *who*," "Write *A* under *mother*") Use symbolic pictures to represent vocabulary. Students mark pictures to show their comprehension. Students do not read yet, and they can only write single letters in English.

Names of Letters in English Use initial letters or written words as memory aids. Teach students to identify sounds of initial consonants, but don't ask students to produce written English or learn spelling rules yet.

2ND GRADE

Description: Students begin to read words in English. At first, the teacher needs to dictate the words the students are reading. With practice, children can read single words or 2-3 word phrases. Pictures are still very important, but now the pictures appear with short words. Children will have problems with English phonetics and spelling, so exercises should include answer boxes. Children can copy the answers from the answer box.

Attention span: about 10 minutes.

38

Continue: All activities from first grade. .

Eliminate: Gradually eliminate desk activities with just crossing out, checking or marking with single letters.

Add: At the beginning of 2nd grade, dictate any written words that you use, so the children can start to relate the familiar sounds to the strange spelling. Gradually introduce recognition and copying of single words or short phrases, usually accompanied by pictures. Memory games using single words or short phrases, "Find Someone Who" games and 7-Up are popular.

3RD-4TH GRADES

Description: Children can read and write whole sentences, and spelling becomes more important as they learn the past tense. Children have more ability in drawing and singing, more knowledge of vocabulary, grammar, reading, writing and spelling in their own language, and more knowledge (telling time, concepts of past, present and future) that teachers can use. Gradually increase emphasis on spelling, grammar and analysis, but always in context, with examples (7-up game) and with a strong emotional content. Continue to use songs, pictures, games, mime/expression/tone of voice, stories, context, etc. New, unfamiliar stories become more popular.

Attention span: 10-15 minutes.

Continue: All activities from 1st and 2nd grades except coloring.

Eliminate: The most infantile songs, stories and games, or activities that children don't like. Coloring is less popular, but drawing is good. Pictures are still fun, but they are not as necessary.

Add: More verbal explanations, definitions and example in English, setting a context using English words, as well as pictures, realia, toys and mime. Hidden words, mazes (labyrinths), pictures with hidden words, crossword puzzles, bingo games, desk activities with whole sentences, pair work and small group work. Activities can be freer, with real interviews or surveys conducted by students. Memory games and "Find Someone Who" games can include complete sentences.

5<u>TH</u>-6<u>TH</u> GRADES

Description: 5th-6th graders are pre-adolescents. Students beginning to enter puberty are more critical of adult authorities and cooperate less with teachers. Teachers and parents lose students' admiration and unquestioning affection. They may criticize society and become fanatical about ecology, politics or religion. 5th and 6th graders demand more autonomy and respect, more choices and more consideration of their individual differences. They can be moody, volatile and very sensitive to any imagined insult. Teachers need to be very delicate and careful to respect their feelings.

Students become more self-conscious, more conscious of their individual differences. They lose the self-confidence that lets them attempt everything and begin to "specialize:" some are recognized by their peers as good artists, musicians, comedians, etc. 5th and 6th grade students lose confidence and enthusiasm for activities that they can't do well. They worry about appearing ridiculous when they draw, sing in front of others, make mistakes, or express their opinions in public. They feel ridiculous when they have to do activities that they consider infantile. 5th and 6th grade students do not like to do games with movements, mime and children's songs, although teachers can perform them.

Popular culture and peers' opinions become more important. They may become very passionate, even fanatical, about some ideology—ecology, religion, human rights or a political issue. Teachers need to listen to students, respect their opinions and give them more autonomy (options about homework, group projects, grading, etc.). Songs should be modern, popular with students. Surveys and contests continue to give an emotional content to English. Analytical games using paper (crosswords, mazes, hidden messages) work well. Students enjoy mystery, fantasy and mythology. Give more individual or small group presentations. Ghost stories, mysteries, fantasy, myths and tales of terror are popular. Students enjoy humor if they control it—don't ridicule students.

Attention span: about 15 minutes.

Continue: Desk activities with whole sentences, using context, definitions and examples in English. Paper games: puzzles, crosswords, hidden words, hidden words with pictures, mazes, bingo, etc. Memory games, "Find Someone Who" games, 7-up, surveys, interviews.

Eliminate: Traditional children's stories, infantile songs, coloring, mime, most active games and finger games. Let the students who are "experts" at drawing, acting, etc. show off their talents, but do not pressure students who feel inadequate in these areas to participate in public.

Add: More humor, parody, especially student-produced. However, teachers should never ridicule students. Increase students' autonomy, choice, free communicative activities, student-designed activities, more small-group work in which each student makes a different individual contribution. Use legends, myths, ghost stories or tales of terror. Songs should be more modern, authentic material, student-selected, or at least student-approved. Reading and writing exercises can imitate or include magazine articles (astrological signs, palm-reading, personality tests, information about pop stars or fashion, sports articles, etc.).

ALL GRADES OF KINDERGARTEN AND PRIMARY SCHOOL:

Give English an emotional content, get students passionate about concepts, using surveys, contests, stories, context, mime/facial expression/tone of voice.

Use contests and competition between different teams to motivate students.

Use positive reinforcement and sincere praise to give students pride in achievement.

Use all senses as much as possible—vision, hearing, touch, taste, smell, movement.

Give all concepts in context, not in an isolated way. Use elements from their experience.

Foment an atmosphere of tolerance and mutual cooperation in the classroom. Do not permit students to ridicule each other.

Never use corporal punishment.

Never lose your temper or scream at students.

At this age, the emotional response of students to English is at least as important as their intellectual progress. Students must feel that learning English is _fun._

TIPS FOR ENGLISH CLASSES WITH KINDERGARTENERS

By Alicia Miranda Arteaga, Outreach and Formation Coordinator, Escuela Pequeño Sol
(Conference given in the UNACH Language School, October 20th, 2004).

In order to begin a workshop, or in this case, an English class, it is necessary to establish a certain atmosphere. Here, this means space, time, patience and appropriate material. "Space" means a physical space, but it is also having "space" in the institutional sense. It is necessary to find an appropriate space in the curriculum, preferably during the first class hours of the morning. "Time" means exactly the right amount of time, which can be no more than 45 minutes, unless this is not just a class but a bilingual education. The materials, prepared beforehand, are vitally important since these are the fundamental tools for implementing your program.

The importance of creating an atmosphere:

The caring atmosphere, which needs to be brought out in the classroom in order to work comfortably, is fundamental. It is necessary to create an atmosphere of mutual trust, keep clear rules, and give all the group members the chance to participate.

A warm atmosphere helps create the appropriate mood.

There are many ways to create the appropriate mood, depending on circumstances, but here I will recommend some tricks that I use in my workshop.

Change places, change classrooms if possible. You can also choose the coziest corner of the classroom, as long as it offers work possibilities.

Play soft music which will announce the beginning of the activity, making sure that it is always the same music, so that the music functions as an announcement that it is time for English class. Rituals are very important for children, so it is good to create routines for them.

Always begin with a greeting, making sure to call each child by his or her name.

After that, use a playful activity (a finger game) to get their attention.

Respect their rhythm. This means that after a concentrated activity, use an active one. Do not try to keep the children sitting down for 45 minutes.

Include creative and artistic activities, songs and games.

Some suggestions for rules, taking into account that the group may need others as well:

When you want to speak, raise your hand.

Don't talk when another classmate is talking.

Speak loudly and clearly so we can hear you.

Treat your classmates well, both boys and girls.

Ask questions.

And enjoy your class.

Sincerely yours,

Alicia Miranda Arteaga

CONCLUSION:

Teachers need to adjust their methods to the age of the students. Younger children are more confident, enthusiastic, affectionate and good at imitation, while older children have more experience and knowledge, analytical ability and reading and writing skills. Each age has its particular advantages, as well as its peculiar difficulties. Good teachers can exploit the abilities of their students and minimize the difficulties if they understand the normal development of children.

Exercises About Children's Development And Lesson Planning

Activity 1

> Identify the problem by letter: A: Not Appropriate for Age; B: Insufficient Balance active /quiet, C: Insufficient Cohesion (E/S/A , recycling); D: Insufficient Detail (specify activities). Write a suggestion for correction.

1. **2nd graders**. E: sing song about body parts. S: students label a picture with names of body parts. A: Team game, sticking body parts onto chart according to T's dictation.

2. **5th/6th graders.** E: Read about verbs with irregular past tenses in books. S: T clarifies reading, helps pairs of SS classify types of irregular verbs. S: Team game; sticking cards with infinitive of verbs onto charts, marked: "--t," "--d," "--ght," "vowel change," and "no change."

3. **Kindergarteners.** E: Sing "Head, Shoulders, Knees and Toes" with movements. S: T tells "The 3 Little Pigs" to teach animal words. S: "Touch Something Red" game.

4. **1st graders.** E: SS listen to "Jack and the Beanstalk" story, imitating T's movements to introduce verbs in past.

S: SS connect words with pictures. A: "The Little Skunk's Hole" song with movements for verbs in past.

5. **3ʳᵈ/4ᵗʰ graders.** E: "The Ants Go Marching One by One" song with movements to present numbers. S: Aerobics with numbers. A: Team game, running to touch numbers on wall according to T's dictation.

6. **1ˢᵗ graders**. E: Sing "Old MacDonald Had a Farm" with movements. S: SS color animals according to T's dictation. A: Team game, sticking animal names onto chart with next to animal pictures.

7. **2ⁿᵈ graders**. E: sing "Today is Monday" using movements, to introduce days of week. S: Crossword puzzle with days. S: T Active Survey-- SS run, stand under words for favorite and least favorite days.

8. **Kindergarteners**. E: Story "The Little Red Hen," T points to pictures of animals. S: SS color animals according to T's dictation. A: T tells story of "The 3 Little Pigs," using puppets.

9. **5ᵗʰ/6ᵗʰ graders.** E: Sing "The Eensy-Weensy Spider" to introduce weather vocabulary. S: SS go to computer lab, find weather words on real online weather forecasts. A: In teams, SS present weather forecasts, creating posters, dramatizations and scripts.

10. **1ˢᵗ graders.** E: Story "Stone Soup," miming food words. S: Color pictures according to T's dictation. A: A food song using movements.

11. **3ʳᵈ/4ᵗʰ graders.** E: "7 Up" to introduce "Did" questions and short answers. S: Desk activity filling in Wh-question words. A: Song "This is the Way the Doctor Works."

12. **2ⁿᵈ graders.** E: Play "Stop!" with verbs. S: Pairs of SS write sentences with verbs.

S: Sing "Can You Swim?"

13. Name 3 strategies Ts can use to communicate instructions in English to beginning SS:

14. Name 2 strategies Ts should AVOID when giving instructions to beginning SS:

15. Name 2 characteristics/activities/situations that are unique to each stage:

Kindergarten, 1ˢᵗ grade, 2ⁿᵈ grade, 5ᵗʰ/6ᵗʰ grades

ACTIVITY 2:

> The following phrases describe which phase
> (Kindergarten, 1st, 2nd, 3rd/4th, 5th/6th)?

* Initial letters (memory aids)

*Circle games

*Enjoy ghost stories, myths, legends

*Spelling starts to be important

*Start Memory games with single words

*Start explanations of grammar/structures

*Individual/small group presentations

*Enjoy repetitious traditional stories

*Most self-confident/energetic

*Recognize letters but can't write

*Critical of teachers, authorities, society

*Start Memory games with single words

*Enjoy magazine articles/questionnaires

*Best pronunciation; no preconceptions

*Most analytical

*Start to use fixed desks

*Peers most important

*Enjoy modern songs; shy about singing

*Begin to learn grammar

*Popular culture important

*Start to identify initial consonants

*Afraid to express opinions in public

*Begin to write sentences

*Options, respect most important

*Start to recognize single words

*Start to mark pictures with single letters

*Need to copy words from answer box

*Desk activities with crossing out/coloring

*Hidden words/mazes/crosswords

*Most recognition of individual differences.

MICROTEACHING 2:

In groups of 3-5 students, plan a class about action verbs for a specific age group. The teacher will assign you the age group.

(Please use the blank pages at the end of each unit for your own notes)

(Please use the blank pages at the end of each unit for your own notes)

UNIT 3: FEEDBACK, TESTING AND GRADING

INTRODUCTION

"How did I do, teacher?" "Can I see my grade?" "Did you like my presentation?" "Did I pronounce that right?" Students need some kind of feedback. Not knowing whether you understood a concept, or whether you pronounced a word correctly, is demoralizing. If students have no idea about their abilities, they can feel insecure and not attempt to use the concepts that they have learned. Feedback gives students confidence to use material that they have mastered, it lets them know when they are ready to try a more difficult task, and it keeps them from assuming responsibilities that they cannot manage yet. It helps them improve in areas where they have problems. Feedback includes gestures, facial expressions, oral or written comments, and test grades.

GESTURES, FACIAL EXPRESSIONS AND COMMENTS

There are many different kinds of feedback. A quick smile and a nod, a grimace that expresses doubt or reservation, a gesture, or a word give students an idea of what they are doing right or wrong. If there is time, a few minutes of chatting can be helpful. Try to include some positive elements in your criticisms of students. Focus on their abilities and effort as well as their problems. Written comments on students' work, notes or letters can help students see how they are doing, where they are doing well and where they need to work more or use different strategies. Teachers can give students a goal to achieve, such as getting information from another student or from a book, or finding out how to do something. The student will be able to assess whether or not he or she was able to achieve the set goals. Students can evaluate each other, or evaluate themselves. Any or all of these methods can be useful for giving students feedback on their work. Students can give teachers feedback with evaluations or informal comments, as well. One of the most common ways for teachers to give students feedback is by grading.

GRADING:

DISADVANTAGES AND ADVANTAGES

Why do teachers grade students? Normally, both students and teachers hate the grading process. For teachers, calculating points and percentages, preparing and grading exams, trying to balance all the relevant areas and information, evaluating ambiguous areas like originality or variety of vocabulary and structures, and summing up something as complex as each student's learning in a number, is difficult at best. It can be traumatic for students, too. So why do it?

Ideally, grading should be feedback, a dialogue between teacher and student, in which both people learn and they both adjust their relationship accordingly. Grades help students improve their learning, identifying priorities and giving each area its proper proportion. Grades help students identify and work on their problem areas, as well as giving students confidence and assurance when they are doing well. Grades give students a realistic idea of their abilities and their mastery of a subject.

HOW TEACHERS CAN USE GRADES

Teachers need to adjust their teaching strategies according to the information that grades can give. If all the students fail an exam, for example, the teacher needs to reevaluate how he or she is teaching the class or preparing the exams. If all the students are getting tens or As, the teacher should consider giving the students a little more difficult material. The teacher needs to use grades as a continual assessment of where the students need more explanation, and where they understand perfectly. The teacher may need to give a second exam or adjust the grading scale if the first exam is a disaster. Then the teacher will have to reassess the teaching and evaluation strategies he or she is using, to avoid further problems.

DETAILED GRADING

As feedback, grades should be detailed, giving the student a precise idea of exactly where he or she has problems. Grades need to be helpful for the students, so they can respond by learning what they need to know. Receiving a 7.3 or a C in a class with no explanation of what was good and what was bad is not very helpful. It is better to divide the grade into different areas, so the student can understand the reasons for the grade. If teachers give specific suggestions for improvement, that makes grades much more useful to the student. If the teacher grades students' corrections or gives students a second opportunity to present a quiz, the grading process becomes a real dialogue, with contributions from both parts

DIFFICULTIES IN GRADING

Although teachers should try to be fair, part of grading is subjective. There are many factors, and it is impossible for a teacher to calculate beforehand exactly how to respond to every eventuality. How do you compare an essay with excellent ideas and ambitious use of language, but that has more grammatical errors, with another essay, which has conventional, superficial ideas, a more timid use of language, but fewer errors? Do you give a student extra points for attempting to use very difficult structures like reported questions, even if the student has problems with them? If you take off points for using words in the native language, what do you do if, for example, you are teaching native Spanish speakers and the student uses a word like "especial"? Is that a word in Spanish or a misspelling of the English word "special"? How about false cognates? Do you accept words like "cuz" for "because", which they see and hear in songs, but which are not used in formal writing? How do you grade something that you suspect came directly from the Internet, but that you can't prove is copied? While teachers do need to cope with these and infinite more difficulties in grading that they may encounter, it is not possible to anticipate them all beforehand.

GRADES AS MOTIVATION OR AS OBSESSION

Grades are also a system of rewards and punishments that teachers can use to motivate students. Students may work harder to achieve a certain grade. Parents may punish children who fail a course, or make them take extra classes. A student who earns good grades is justifiably proud, if he or she feels that the grade reflects hard work and interest. For this reason, grades must be fair and impartial. But there is often too much emphasis on grades. When grades become an obsession, learning suffers. Grades cannot be a kind of feedback if it becomes vitally important for the student to get only As or 10s. In this case, it is impossible for the teacher to use grades as suggestions for improvement. The obsession with grades stifles intellectual curiosity, experimentation and originality. The material stops being interesting for itself, and becomes just a way of obtaining good grades.

GRADES TO DEMONSTRATE IMPORTANCE OF WORK

Grades are a way that teachers can show students what their priorities are. If the teacher tells students to correct their work, but doesn't grade the corrections, students will feel that correction is not important. If teachers grade only on language use and not on content, students will learn that only form matters, while substance, the communication of ideas, is irrelevant. If each of the 4 areas (listening, speaking, reading and writing) receives an equal proportion in teachers' evaluations, students learn that speaking is as important as writing.

GRADES AS A LEARNING EXPERIENCE

Teachers need to make grades a learning experience. They need to review any quizzes or exams with the students. If students can correct their work, they will learn from their mistakes. Students should feel free to ask questions about their mistakes, and teachers need to take a little time to give any extra explanations that are necessary.

(See Jeremy Harmer's *The Practice of English Language Teaching,* Chapter 7, also Chapter 8, section 10 of Jim Scrivener's *Learning Teaching,* published by MacMillan Heinemann in 1994.)

TESTING

Testing should not be traumatic for children. It is more important for young children to learn that English is fun and not too difficult than it is for them to learn specific vocabulary and structures. Part of what you teach them is confidence in their own abilities. You may not want to test kindergarten students at all. But usually elementary schools will insist that you test your students.

USING ENGLISH IN TEST INSTRUCTIONS

It is important to use English in tests. Students will notice the inconsistency if you tell them that it is important to use and understand English in the class, and then give them exams that stress translation into their native language, or that give instructions in the native language. At the same time, it is important to make sure that your students understand and can follow your directions.

MODELING AND PREPARATION BEFORE TESTS

Any test instructions you plan to use, you need to practice with your students before the real exam day. Do an exercise in class together, first. Make a large copy of the exercise, stick it on the board, and do it in front of the class, with all the students copying what you do (coloring, crossing out pictures, writing letters under the pictures, etc.). Then let them do a similar exercise with no modeling from you. Finally, give them another similar exercise as a test. Give students examples in each section of your tests, so they can see what you want. One way to make sure that students understand your testing technique is to use the same techniques in exercises before you test them. Give the students pretests or quizzes for practice before you give them an exam. This gives the students more confidence. It also helps the teacher work out any problems with his or her testing technique and make sure that the instructions are clear.

Another technique is to give students double quizzes, using one for practice and the other for improvement. Teachers help students correct their mistakes, students take home their corrected quizzes to study, and then take a slightly different version of the quiz, using the same techniques but varying the order or wording of the questions. This gives students a chance to learn from their mistakes. The teacher can ask the students to save their quizzes in a folder or to stick them in their notebooks so the students can use them as a study guide. If the teacher observes that many students didn't understand a certain concept, he or she can explain it again in a different way before repeating the quiz.

TESTING CHILDREN OF DIFFERENT AGES

KINDERGARTEN STUDENTS: Kindergarteners can't write yet. You can evaluate them just by observation, through games or activities, or test them by asking them to color pictures according to your oral instructions ("Color the cat blue. Color the dog red."). You can draw rows with 4 or 5 pictures in each row and have them cross out the one you indicate. You can ask kindergarteners to complete a picture with drawings ("Draw a dog under the table. Draw a book on the table."), but you have to be careful not to exceed their abilities. They can't do complicated drawings, and they often have trouble understanding spatial concepts like "in front of" and "behind."

The test in the picture above is a test on the questions: "How many?" "What?" "What time?" "Who?" "How much?" "How old?" "When?" "Where?" and "What color?" This test could be used for kindergarten or for first grade. The teacher's oral instructions for kindergarteners could be: "Look at row 1. Find 'What?' Color 'What?' green. Find 'What time?' Color 'What time?' blue. Find 'How many?' Color 'How many?' red." The kindergarten teacher could also use other techniques, such as: "Cross out 'What time?'" or "Circle 'How many?'"

1ST GRADERS: First graders can use the same techniques (coloring, crossing out, circling) as kindergarteners. In addition, you can give them a row of pictures and ask them to write a single letter, A, B, C or D, under each picture. ("Write A under 'What time?'. Write B under 'How many?'") You can write the letters on the board at the same time so the students can copy them easily. Practice this technique with them a few times so they understand it well.

2ND GRADERS: For 2nd graders, use rows of pictures again, but now give them whole words in a box to one side. Have the students copy the correct word under each picture. You can gradually change from single words to phrases and longer sentences. Don't put more than 4-5 pictures in each row so the students won't be confused. 2nd graders often have problems copying words with correct spelling. Be flexible with them at first, until they become accustomed to English spelling. Another testing technique is to give students a selection of answers that they need to match with the appropriate question. You can have students match words with pictures or well-known names, too. ("Homer Simpson—father. Lisa—sister.")

The following picture is a test for second graders about the same question words. The questions and answers are simple phrases and single words, with pictures to help the students understand.

Name _____ 2nd grade

CIRCLE

Who?	$20.00 pesos	8:00	on Monday	[face] Paty
What?	6	a car	in the closet	7:00
How much?	I'm six	yellow	$5 pesos	in November
How old?	green	David	on Thursday	I'm seven
How many?	20	on the bed	Ana	blue
When?	an apple	$10 pesos	in April	a dog
Where?	under the table	9:00	14	Jose
What time?	$10 pesos	10:00	I'm 7	on the chair
What color?	a fish	8	red	13

3RD -4TH GRADERS: 3rd and 4th graders can read entire sentences. Teachers need to concentrate more on spelling with 3rd and 4th graders, since often the only difference between the past and present tense of verbs is one letter. Tests can continue to use matching and writing answers under pictures or well-known names. Students of this age can also use true-false or fill-in-the-blanks tests. Have them fill in a verb from a list in a sentence where the context is very clear. ("We eat pizza. We drink milk.")

70

Name _____ 3rd/4th grade

Write a word from the box in the space.

_____ is that? - He's the director.

_____ apples are there? - There are six.

_____ are you? - I'm nine.

_____ is the party? - On Saturday.

_____ is the book? - On the bed.

_____ is it? - It's ten o'clock.

_____ is that? - It's a pen.

_____ is that? - It's green.

_____ is that? - It's five pesos.

when
who
How many
How old
what time
How much
What color
where
what

5TH -6TH GRADERS: Older children do not need to choose answers from a box of options. They may enjoy putting the question words into a fun context, like an interview with Shakira, or writing more personalized answers for the question words. Two tests for 5th and 6th graders appear on the next pages:

71

Name_____ 6th grade

Complete the T.V. reporter's conversation with Shakira.

Reporter: "_____ your name?" Shakira: "My name's Shakira."

R: "_____ are you from?" S: "I'm from Colombia.

R: "_____ are you?" S: "I'm twenty eight years old."

R: "_____ is that?" S: "He's my manager."

R: "_____ CDs do you have?" S: "19 singles and 3 albums."

R: "_____ is your hair?" S: "Blonde—today!"

R: "_____ are the tickets to your concert?" S: "50 dollars."

R: "_____ is your favorite musical style?" S: "Salsa!"

R: "Thank you, Shakira. This is T.V. Azteca news."

_____

72

Name_____ 6th grade

How many brothers and sisters do you have?

_____

Where do you go for vacations?

_____

What is your favorite food?

_____

When do you have music class?

_____

What time do you get up?

_____

How much does a chocolate bar cost?

_____

Who is your favorite musician?

_____

What color do you like best?

_____

How old are you?

_____

It is easy to give 5th and 6th grade students specific questions about reading or listening comprehension, as well as grammar and vocabulary. Again, the questions should be in English. Use questions that really test their comprehension. Use question words like "what," "how," "who," "where," and especially, "why." Don't ask questions they can answer with an isolated word without understanding the main idea. "Why did the girl invite the bear home?" "Who helped the little dog?" are good questions. For 5th and 6th grade students, short essays or stories are harder to grade but more fun for students to write. Use them as part of your exam, if you want, or give essays at another time.

ORAL EXAMS

Oral exams are very difficult to give to a class of 25 or more students. Don't test them alone or in pairs while the rest of the class waits, getting bored and restless. You can test their oral abilities discreetly while they work in groups or play games.

PROBLEMS IN TEST DESIGN

Make sure that your tests really test language. Matching similar figures or coloring a picture in normal, expected colors doesn't test children's vocabulary. The children can do these activities even if they don't understand any English at all. Avoid questions that are too easy, or that have obvious answers. Questions should not be too difficult, either. Ambiguous questions have too many possible answers so it is difficult to grade a test with these questions. Interdependent or sequential questions also cause problems. If children can't answer the first question correctly, they will get the subsequent questions wrong, too. For example, if a child makes a spelling mistake in a crossword puzzle, that error will affect all the other words in the puzzle.

EXTRA ACTIVITIES FOR STUDENTS WHO FINISH QUICKLY

Children get bored if they finish a test before the rest of the class. Prepare activities for them to do while they wait for their classmates to finish. The activity can be as simple as drawing on the back of the exam. You can give the quicker students pictures to color, story books to read, or puzzles or mazes to resolve, while the slower students finish their tests. However, although puzzles, hidden words, scrambled words, crosswords and mazes are fun extra activities, do not use them as tests. Some children have a lot of natural ability in solving puzzles while others do not. Puzzles test children's puzzle solving ability, not their English.

H	W	A	R	E	T	H	E	R	E
C	E	R	H	W	H	O	S	E	N
U	M	E	O	H	O	W	H	K	E
M	I	R	W	Y	W	H	I	C	H
W	T	E	L	H	O	W	E	I	W
O	T	H	O	W	F	A	R	S	H
H	A	T	N	H	T	H	E	W	E
O	H	S	G	A	E	W	H	O	R
M	W	I	H	T	N	H	W	H	E
W	H	O	W	M	A	N	Y	T	W

5th-6th Grade:

Hidden Words ↑↓→

How?	How?	How many?	How much?
How far?	How long?	How far?	How sick?
How often?	Is there?	Are there?	What time?
Why?	Who?	Who?	
Whose?	When?	What?	
Where?	Where?	Which?	

Clues are on the next page. Squares with an X through them are the spaces between words in a two-word answer.

Across

1. Q: _____ socks do you prefer? A: The red ones.
4. Q: _____ you mind sitting down? A: Of course not.
7. Q: ___ ___ are you? A: I will be 7 on Tuesday!
9. Q: ___ ___ sisters do you have? A: 3, and 1 brother
12. Q: ___ did you get here? A: By bicycle.
14. Q: ___ _____ do you brush your teeth? A: Twice a day!
15. Q: ___ it rain tomorrow? A: Probably.
17. Q: ___ she eaten breakfast yet? A: No, she hasn't.
18. Q: ___ you swim? A: Yes, I can swim very well.
20. Q: _____ are you from? A: I'm from Tuxtla.
21. Q: _____ your book? A: It's on my desk!
23. Q: _____ is your birthday? A: June 9th
24. Q: ___ you an architect? A: No, I'm a student.
25. Q: _____ your mother work? A: Yes, she's a teacher

Down

2. Q: ___ _____ does it cost? A: $5.00
3. Q: ___ _____ any milk? A: No, we need to buy more.
5. Q: _____ your name? A: Marcela
6. Q: ___ is he sad? A: Because he got a 5 in science.
8. Q: ___ you like pizza? A: Yes, I love it!
9. Q: ___ _____ did they chat? A: For 3 hours!
10. Q: ___ ___ the tallest? A: Juan.
11. Q: ___ _____ any letters for me? A: Yes, there are.
13. Q: ___ _____ is your new car? A: Black.
15. Q: ___ _____ is the party? A: At 9 o'clock.
16. Q: ___ your father tall? A: No, he's short and fat.
19. Q: _____ is this sweater? A: It's Pepe's.
22. Q: _____ you finished your homework? A: Yes
23. Q: _____ did you do? A: I ran away.

MATHEMATICS FOR TEACHERS : CALCULATING NUMERIC GRADES

THE RULE OF 3: The easiest technique for obtaining the grade is to divide, using "the rule of three." Put an extra zero after the number of correct answers. Then divide this number by the total answers to get the grade. For example, if the student got 23 correct answers on a test with 25 questions, divide 230 by 25. $25 \div 230 = 9.2$. The student's grade is 9.2.

POINTS PER QUESTION: Another technique for finding the grade is to divide 10 by the number of answers on your test. That gives you the point value of each question. For example, in a test with 25 possible answers, you divide 10 by 25 possible answers. $10 \div 25 = 0.4$ points for each question. Multiply the correct answers times 0.4 to get the grade. If the student got 23 correct answers, multiply $23 \times 0.4 = 9.2$. An answer that is only half right would give the student 0.2 points in a test with 25 answers—half the value of a totally right answer. If all the answers are right, the student gets 10 points total. For example, 5 questions are worth 2 points each, 10 questions are worth 1 point

80

each, 20 questions are worth 0.5 points each, 25 questions are worth 0.4 points each, and 50 questions are worth 0.2 points each. Plan your tests to include 5, 10, 20, 25 or 50 answers, to keep the mathematics simple. If your test has a number of answers that you cannot multiply to get exactly 10 (12 answers, for example), you will have to multiply each answer by a mixed number. If you have 12 questions, 10 ÷ 12 = 0.833, you must give 0.833 points for each answer. You can round the number off and give each answer 8.5 points in this case.

COMMENTS AS MOTIVATORS

Although you will probably give number or letter grades to your students, a written comment by the teacher will motivate students very much. If you have time, try to write comments occasionally, especially on work where the students express their own feelings.

AVERAGES:

You will need to calculate averages in order to give your students a final grade. To do this, first add all their grades. Then divide the result by the number of quizzes or assignments they did. If your students do 7 homework assignments, for example, with grades of 7.3, 5.2, 8.4, 10, 10, 3.4, and 9.2, you add those grades up: 7.3 + 5.2 + 8.4 + 10 + 10 + 3.4 + 9.2 = 53.5 total. Divide the 53.5 total by the 7 homework assignments, 53.5 ÷ 7 = 7. 64. Rounded off, the average is 7.6.

DISTRIBUTION OF GRADES

If you decide to give 50% of the grade to quizzes, 20% to homework and 30% to a presentation, how do you calculate the final grade? Calculate the average for each element: quizzes, homework and presentation, then multiply them by their proportionate worth. In this case, since the quizzes are worth 50% of the grade, multiply that number by 5. Multiply the homework average by 2 and the presentation average by 3. This gives you the final grade as a percentage, based on 100. You can divide this result by 10 (just move the decimal point one place to the left) to get the grade on a 0-10 scale.

CONCLUSION

Teachers need to give children non-verbal, oral and written feedback to give the children confidence and an accurate idea about their progress. Testing and grading, however, are polemical issues. Some authors insist that children should take standardized tests to assess their learning, as well as the English program of the school. Other authors state that young children do not understand the concept of testing so the results are inaccurate.

FOR MORE INFORMATION

See the following articles online:

"Testing Young Children," in *Head, Shoulders, Knees, and all that, a blog about early childhood education*, October 21, 2006
http://simplesongs.blogs.com/head_shoulders_knees_and_/childhood_education_policy

"Issues of Assessment in Testing Children Under Age Eight," Gwen G. Stevens and Karen DeBord, in *The Forum of Family and Consumer Issues*, NC State University, Volume 6, Number 2, Spring 2001
http://www.ces.ncsu.edu/depts/fcs/pub/w001sp/stevens.html

"English Proficiency Test: The Oral Component of a Primary School", by Ishbel Hingle and Viv Linington, *Forum Online Journal of English Teaching*, Volume 35, Number 2, June 1997   http://exchanges.state.gov/englishteaching/forum-journal.html

*"Standardized Tests For Young Children? Not Yet!!" ACEI, *"On Standardized Testing: A Position Paper of the Association for Childhood Education International."* *Childhood Education.* Spring, 1991. pg. 130-142.

MICROTEACHING 3:

Plan a short lesson about a specific structure or set of vocabulary, designed for children at a particular level. (This time, plan for children of a different age from the children you used in your previous microteaching.) At the end of your lesson, you will give your classmates a test on the material. First model the method you will use, explain the test and give the instructions. Then hand out the test. Plan an activity for the fastest students to do while the slower students finish the test. Collect the tests, grade them, and then calculate the average grade for the group.

EXERCISES:

Calculate the grades below. Show the process used to calculate the answers.

1. Carlos got 13 correct answers on a test with 30 questions. What is Carlos's grade, out of a possible 10 points? Include 1 number after the decimal point

2. Ben got 13 correct answers on a test with 25 questions. What is Ben's grade, out of a possible 10 points? Include 1 number after the decimal point.

3. Ava's grades this month were: 7.4, 8.3, 9.6, 6.2 and 5. What is her average for the month, out of a possible 10 points? Include 1 number after the decimal point.

4. Tony's grades were 5.4, 0, 9.1, 8.6 and 7.0. What is his average for the month, out of a possible 10 points? Include 1 number after the decimal point

5. Homework is worth 20% of the grade, Presentations are worth 30 percent and Exams are worth 50%. Rodrigo got 4.8 on his homework, a 9.5 on his presentation, and a 6.4 in his exam. What is his final grade, out of 10 points? Include 1 number after the decimal point.

86

> The following tests contain errors or problems.
>
> State why the test is inappropriate.

6. The teacher gives the 1st grade class a game in which groups of students color different pieces of clothing in specific colors. ("Color the shirt red.") One group argues about whether to color the shirt red or green. The teacher tells them that either one is fine.

7. The teacher gives 1st graders a fill-in-the-blank test. The answers are written in a box, and the students have to copy the correct answer under a picture.

8. The teacher gives 2nd grade students a test where they color pictures of body parts in different colors, according to the teacher's dictation.

9. The teacher gives 6th graders a test about animals, using a crossword puzzle.

10. The teacher dictates letters for the kindergarten students to write under the picture of each profession.

11. The teacher gives 1st graders a test on verbs, telling the students to cross out the picture for "run," circle the picture for "jump," tick the picture for "swim," and underline the picture for "fly."

12. The teacher gives kindergarteners a test on foods, dictating the instructions: "Ok, now we are going to have a test about foods. I want you to get out your crayons, now. So, you have to color the picture of the apple with your yellow crayon."

13. The first graders' test has written instructions: "Write A under the car. Write B under the bus. Write C under the bicycle. Write D under the shoes."

14. In multiple choice tests, how many answers should a teacher include for each question?   Why?

15. How many questions total are usually included in a test? Why?

88

(Please use the blank pages at the end of each unit for your own notes)

(Please use the blank pages at the end of each unit for your own notes)

UNIT 4: CONTROL OF THE GROUP

INTRODUCTION

One of the most difficult problems for new teachers is keeping control of the class. Group control can be especially difficult with young children. Most young children have very little motivation to learn English, and getting good grades is not very important to them. They have little self-control, so if they want to play, scream or fight right now, they can cause problems for the teacher.

Many new teachers begin their first job with the idea that they will be friends with the students. These new teachers may try to avoid disciplining their students. The students sense when new teachers have no control, and they will test the limits of those teachers' tolerance. You are not your students' friend. They already have friends. You are their teacher. You can be friendly, but you are the authority. Your students will not learn if you cannot control the group, they will not have fun and they can even hurt their classmates. A dynamic, interesting, fun class needs to have rules, just as a football game has rules. You need to be the referee, and you need to inspire respect as well as affection.

Use EFFECTIVE STRATEGIES FOR EACH KEY MOMENT IN GROUP CONTROL

Four key moments in group control are:

A. At the beginning of the course: when you establish class rules and begin to create a positive atmosphere in your classroom.

B. When you plan the activities for your next lesson(s).

C. During the class: keeping your students engaged.

D. When problems start.

Strategies for each key moment follow.

A) AT THE BEGINNING OF THE COURSE

1) MAKE YOUR EXPECTATIONS CLEAR.

Tell children what you expect from them. No one is born knowing how to behave in class. **Tell them what you want them to do, and why.** Discuss everyone's expectations for the course with the students. Working together, decide on a short list of rules to make the class more effective. Use positive language (*"Use English in class"* instead of *"Don't* *use Spanish."*). Discuss with the students what consequences should result from breaking the rules, for example: "Anyone who speaks Spanish in class has to pay a fine of one peso. We will use the money to have a party the last day of the course." Don't accept drastic consequences, such as automatically failing the course, because you won't be able to enforce them. When everyone is satisfied with the rules and their consequences, put a written copy of these rules in a prominent place as a reference. You can point to the rules every time you correct students to remind them that everyone participated in establishing these rules and their consequences.

2) CREATE A POSITIVE ATMOSPHERE IN THE CLASSROOM.

Get to know your students individually. It is especially important to learn your students' names as soon as possible. During the first few days of class you can write a description of each student in your notebook for reference, take photos of the students and make an album with their names and photos, ask the students to wear name tags, make a seating chart or put name tags on their desks to help you learn those names. Use their names every time you talk with them, to show your respect and to practice their names. Find out as much information as you can about them: their preferences, their hopes, their family situations. Learn to love, respect, recognize and appreciate each student for their own unique qualities. Accept your students as they are; discover the good qualities of your difficult students.

Students behave better and learn better when they feel loved and appreciated. They will not want to make you sad or angry if they like you. Compliment them on their clothes, toys or hairstyles. Give them **positive reinforcement.** Notice what they do well, and express your appreciation of them. Show an interest in their activities.

It is especially important to **express your appreciation and love for difficult students.** Often, a difficult student has low self-esteem. Your expressions of affection will help that student accept himself, and so behave well. **Give children a lot of attention**, especially when they are behaving well. Often children behave badly in order to get attention. If they get lots of attention for being good, they won't need to misbehave. **Use hugs, pats on the back, positive physical contact** to show them that you like them, or to reassure them. Sometimes holding a very aggressive or violent child in your lap and rocking him will quiet the child and make him feel safe and loved. His aggression will dissipate. At the same time, you can continue with your class, singing or talking with the rest of the group.

Analyze the students' motivations, and try to give them legitimate ways to attain their goals. Children have natural and real needs: for attention, for communication, and for movement. Those desires are not bad—they are normal. The children need to know that it is ok to want attention, to want to talk or to move. As a teacher, you need to find ways to help children get what they want. If a child is stealing things or tormenting another student because he wants attention, show him that he can get attention in positive ways. Make him your official assistant, letting him pass out the papers, erase the board, or help you in the classroom. Praise him for being such a good helper. If he wants to talk, reassure him that he will be able to talk at recess, or let him pass notes—in English. If your students are restless, give them an activity or game with movements, mime or finger games. Show them that you understand and accept their "dark side," that you don't hate them when they feel uncooperative or sad. Help them channel their anger or sadness in legitimate ways.

Be friendly, but authoritative. Establish a positive class atmosphere of tolerance, patience and respect, modeling the behavior and attitudes you want students to have. If you want children to be tolerant with each other and not ridicule each other, you must follow the same rules. Explain to your students the importance of accepting each other and being tolerant, even when their classmates make mistakes. Tell them that aggression, discrimination and ridicule are not acceptable in your classroom. Tell them clearly, without making them feel bad, how other people feel when they are ridiculed or attacked in class. Explain to them why you will not tolerate aggression or ridicule in your classroom.

Use stories. Remember that small children have difficulty imagining other people's perspectives. Use stories, fables, parables and anecdotes to teach moral lessons. These stories help children feel emotionally, as well as understand intellectually, why they shouldn't do something. Stories help teach people empathy for others, show positive attitudes and teach the consequences of bad behavior. You can invent stories especially to talk about the problems you encounter in the group (racism, cruelty, ridicule, laziness, etc.). Make the stories interesting or funny, but use them to teach the morals that you want the class to learn.

Model the behavior you want. If you want children to be tolerant with each other and not ridicule each other, you must follow the same rule. Praise children who are behaving the way you want, and **use them as an example** for the others.

Discuss with the group options they can use when they are attacked or offended. There are alternatives to the obvious and unacceptable strategies of hitting or insulting their attackers. Help the children understand they can tell other students to leave them alone, or explain to other children what they don't like. They can stop playing with a child who is bothering them, or tell the teacher, instead of fighting.

3) CULTIVATE A FRIENDLY, ACCEPTING PERSONALITY

Examine your attitudes towards students and towards yourself as a teacher. Perfectionism and intolerance, towards yourself or your students, will make you bad-tempered and frustrated.

Express your own sense of humor and playfulness with children. Enjoy yourself, get in touch with your own inner child, and enjoy your students. If you enjoy playing or joking, have fun with your children, and they will enjoy your classes. Don't be embarrassed to be childish. That is your best entry into the world of your students. Laugh at their jokes and humor, too.

B. PLAN INTERESTING CLASSES: BORED STUDENTS =
PROBLEM STUDENTS

The same techniques you learned in Unit 1: The ABCs of Class Planning, are also important for keeping control of the group. When you plan, anticipate behavior problems in each of the following areas.

AGE-APPROPRIATE: Design classes that are appropriate for the students' age, abilities, level and learning style. Respect developmental differences; teach concepts that students are capable of understanding. Adapt your lesson to your particular students: their interests and family context. Frustrated or bored students often behave badly; students who feel successful usually behave well.

BALANCED: Use a variety of activities (whole group/teams/small groups/pairs/individual; visual/auditory/kinesthetic; active/quiet;). Students who cannot use their excess energy often become restless and behave badly. Young students cannot sit quietly for half an hour, so give them an energetic activity to channel their energy. Keep them moving until they are exhausted. Then they will be quiet and ready to learn. Use **pacing** (changing activities often, keeping the rhythm of the class fast) to keep students interested. **Change activities** every 5-10 minutes with kindergarteners, every 15-20 minutes with 5th or 6th graders.

COHERENT: Students will cooperate more if you capture their attention at the beginning of the class, if they understand the new language presented, and if they can play with this new material. Use the Engagement/Study/Activation format correctly. Do not begin the class with a long explanation. Your Engagement must be interesting, your Study should be clear and your Activation participative and fun.

DETAILED: Plan carefully. Memorize the words of any songs or stories you will use, learn the rules to the games and practice the activities before class. Anticipate possible problems and plan strategies to resolve them. Plan abundant activities: enough to change every 5 minutes, with a few extra activities for students who finish quickly or for emergencies, as well as a few boring alternatives which you can use as necessary as a disciplinary measure. Don't pause between activities. **Bored students usually behave badly. Keep students occupied.** Give students who finish one activity quickly another quiet activity to entertain them while their classmates are finishing.

ENGLISH: Use simple, repetitive language and short sentences; illustrate your meaning with mime, gestures, facial, corporal and vocal expression, as well as with pictures, toys, realia and examples, to motivate students, showing them that they can really understand English. However, you can translate occasional words or phrases if students are still confused. Do not frustrate or confuse children with complex language, long sentences or too much unfamiliar vocabulary.

FUN: Use interesting techniques: games, pictures, mime, songs and stories, to keep students interested. Choose options that students will enjoy more (repetitious songs rather than a spoken repetition drill, competitive games to check answers to homework). Use humor and playfulness. Plan your lessons the way you would plan a dinner menu: with variety, appeal, and value. If you are having fun with the students, they will usually enjoy the class and cooperate with you.

C) KEEP STUDENTS ENGAGED.

BE SENSITIVE TO THE ATMOSPHERE OF THE CLASS, and change activities the moment you sense that the students are becoming bored. If the students are restless and want to move, start an active game. If they are tired, give them a quiet activity. Don't wait until students are getting bored with one activity before you change. Change while most of the students are still excited about the activity, when they still want more. Change activities the moment that students begin to look bored. Modify your plans according to students' responses. Let students decide between alternative activities. Spend more time if students are confused; eliminate explanations if students understand quickly.

USE ROUTINES (PHYSICAL, VERBAL OR MUSICAL), to get students back into synchronization and working together. These routines could include finger games, sequences of movements, rhymes, chants or songs. Routines concentrate students' attention, channel their energy and get them all on the same track.

USE PEER PRESSURE to keep children cooperative. Peer pressure is when the expectations of your equals (classmates, friends or colleagues) obligate you to behave well. Children can enforce good behavior by their classmates. Techniques using peer pressure can include: giving the class collective rewards, such as a favorite activity, or taking those rewards away; organizing competitive team games or competitions between groups, taking away points from the whole team for individual bad behavior; or asking students to evaluate their classmates' presentations, voting for the best work. You can then give prizes to the students with the most votes in an "Oscar Awards Ceremony."

INVOLVE DISTRACTED STUDENTS IN THE CLASS. Ask questions to the whole group first, so all the students will feel involved. Then call on the distracted students or the students who are talking, using their names to bring their attention back to the class. Ask these students questions or elicit their opinions or experiences related to the topic. Invite them to participate in an encouraging, respectful way, so that they do not suspect your manipulation. Stand next to distracted students, touch them on the shoulder.

D. SOLVE BEHAVIOR PROBLEMS QUICKLY.

1) REMOVE DISTRACTIONS. Deal with distraction or minor problems immediately. It is much better to prevent problems than to discipline badly behaved students who are already causing problems. Act to prevent or resolve minor problems quickly, before they become serious. If a child is constantly playing with a toy, iPod or cell phone and not paying attention, remove the object and tell the child you will return it after class. If the whole group often becomes distracted, place children boy-girl-boy-girl, away from their closest friends, so they aren't tempted to talk. If two children are constantly talking and bothering each other, offer them the alternative: they can work quietly together, or you will move one or both of them to another seat. A good teacher controls the class in subtle ways, so that students are not aware of the manipulation, and almost never needs to use discipline.

2) GIVE STUDENTS THEIR CHOICE OF ACCEPTABLE ALTERNATIVES

Give children the choice between 2 options. You design and control the options; they choose which one they want. For example: "If you cooperate and don't cheat, we can continue playing this game. Or do you prefer doing the exercise on page 37 of your books?" "Do you want to move over to Ana's table, or can you be quiet where you are?" "Would you like to sing "The Ants Go Marching" or would you like to do aerobics with numbers?" The two options obviously do not include undisciplined behavior, so when the students choose one option, they automatically have to behave correctly. Giving students options makes them feel more involved in the class, because they make the decisions, but since the teacher controls the possible outcomes, he or she only offers options that will create a productive lesson.

3) USE REWARDS TO MOTIVATE STUDENTS.

Promise children picture cards, favorite games or stories if they cooperate in a specific way. Tell students that you will give them conditional rewards (favorite activities, stamps or pictures stories, etc.) if they cooperate, finish their class work or bring in their homework. **Make the conditions for getting the reward clear.** Show the students that **the reward is the natural consequence of their good behavior, and not a special favor from the teacher. Rewards must be immediate and consistent.** You can use rewards like a dessert at the end of a meal—if you finish the activities you need to do, then we will all have time for a game or story.

For individual students, bring small pictures or stamps as a reward. They can collect the pictures, color them or exchange a certain number of stamps for a large poster. Group rewards could be doing a favorite activity, hearing a story, playing a game or singing a favorite song. Group rewards are especially effective, since they will promote peer pressure to behave.

MONSTER CARDS AS REWARDS

Most children like funny pictures on cards that they can collect. This book includes some cards, but you can also make your own "monsters," or ask your students to help you. Fold a blank sheet of paper into 4 equal parts vertically, then into 4 equal parts horizontally. You will have 16 equal squares. Write the vocabulary you want at the bottom of each square. Then draw a funny picture in the square that will help students remember the words. Photocopy pages of "monster pictures," cut the copies into individual cards, and give them to the students as a stimulus, as rewards and as memory aids. Give out cards generously, like candy. In fact, cards work in the same way that candy does, but cards are cheaper for the teacher and don't affect the children's health.

108

Shirt
monster

blouse monster

skirt monster

pants monster

Socks
monsters

underwear
monster

boots monster

shoes
monsters

sweater monster

dress monster

shorts monster

jacket monster

hat monster

jeans monster

coat monster

T-shirt monster

Monster cards work as prizes for the winning student or the winning team in a game. You can use cards to reward each child who participates in a song or activity. When you ask children to open their books to a certain page, identify the first complete row of children to find the page, and give each child in that row a card. The other children will try to find the page more quickly the next time. Cards can help teachers control the group. If some children's talking or behavior interrupts your class, take cards away from those children. Younger children enjoy coloring the cards, while older children like to collect and exchange them. When children collect 25 or 50 cards, the teacher can exchange them for a larger poster with every "monster" in the series.

4. TAKE AWAY REWARDS FOR BAD BEHAVIOR. One of the best disciplinary techniques is deprivation of an anticipated reward. If children behave badly, take rewards away from them. Interrupt a fun activity and substitute an unattractive option. Tell a noisy group that you can't continue a fun activity with them because they are not cooperating. Stop telling the story, suspend the game and give them a repetition drill or a boring written exercise until they promise to behave. Tell children that cheating in a game or interrupting will make it impossible for the group to play. Then, after a warning or two, interrupt the activity, and give them another, more structured and boring. Exclude individual students who behave badly from games or move them to a different chair away from friends. Take away the picture cards you gave the child as a reward. (Make sure that you give children enough rewards so that you can take them away if necessary!) This strategy is very effective if you are consistent and keep your word. Never threaten to take away a reward if you can't really do it. Students may test you by behaving badly to see if you really mean what you say. You must be consistent.

5) USE SILENCE TO OBTAIN SILENCE. Lower your voice when students are too noisy. Interrupt yourself in the middle of a sentence, fold your arms, look severely at the students who are talking most loudly, and wait silently for them to finish. It doesn't matter if it takes a few minutes. Just stop talking—preferably in the middle of a sentence. The other students will notice, and they will usually tell the noisy children to be quiet. Never shout. Lower your voice, so the students need to be quiet in order to hear you. Model the quiet voice you want them to use.

DISCIPLINE: THE LAST RESORT

When none of the techniques above have worked, the teacher must apply fair, consistent, impersonal, immediate and brief disciplinary action. Although disciplining the entire group is unfair, occasional use of this technique can create peer pressure on difficult students.

DISCIPLINE SHOULD BE IMMEDIATE AND CONSISTENT.

Be effective, consistent and firm in discipline. If you promise a reward or a disciplinary action, you must give it. If you tell a child that you will exclude him from the game if he hits his classmate again, you need to enforce that rule instantly. Small children have a short attention span. Discipline or rewards at the end of the week or month is too far away for them to imagine. For this reason, notes to parents are not very effective. In addition, parents may defend their child against you.

DISCIPLINE MUST BE CLEAR.

Be fair to students. Do not punish a student for ignorance. Only discipline a student who is violating a rule that you have already given to the class, and that the students understand. **Make sure the child understands why he is being punished.** Sometimes children think that you are punishing them for an innocent activity, like asking questions or making honest mistakes. **Give students a chance to defend themselves.** Do not discipline a child without letting the child explain his actions. If you discipline a child and then discover that you made a mistake, apologize immediately and publicly to the child. Preferably talk privately with the student after class, instead of confronting him publicly.

SHOW THAT YOU ACCEPT THE CHILDREN, BUT NOT THEIR BAD BEHAVIOR.

Children may feel that you punish them because you hated them. Don't tell children that they are bad people, stupid or uncooperative. They may believe you, and become the kind of people you describe. Just explain, in a calm, cool way, that the bad action was unacceptable and has caused a consequence that they don't like.

DISCIPLINE FUNCTIONS AS A MODEL FOR OTHER CHILDREN.
Children need to see what will happen if they are bad.
Often, when one child is disciplined, the others behave
better. But keep the disciplinary action brief and
impersonal. Too much time spent on disciplining one
student will result in losing control of the rest of the group.

DISCIPLINARY TECHNIQUES

1) EXPLANATION AND REFLECTION.

**Discipline should be part of the teaching-learning
process, making the student reflect on what he/did.** Put
the badly behaved child away from the others, in a special
chair or in the corner, and then ignore him. He can think
about what he has done, and return to the group when he
is ready to behave well. You can turn your back to the
badly-behaved child and organize a favorite activity for the
others, in which he is not included. Don't respond to him
while he is behaving badly.

Create a "thinking corner." Send the furious child
(kindergarten through 2nd grade) to a quiet corner of the
room, facing the wall. Give the child crayons and paper to

calm down, and let the child recover serenity or think about the problem. At the same time, give the rest of the class a favorite activity. The isolated child in the "thinking corner" cannot participate until he/she apologizes or promises to behave. When the child announces that he/she is ready to cooperate, the teacher welcomes the child back into the group.

Older children might talk with you or write an essay for extra homework about their motives, their unacceptable actions, and what they will do in the future.

If you have a student who is consistently difficult, discuss the problem with the child and make a contract with him/her, in which you both decide together what will be acceptable behavior, and what the consequences of bad behavior will be.

2) EXTRA HOMEWORK

For older students (3rd-6th grades), extra homework can be an effective disciplinary action. Like all disciplinary actions, this should be used rarely, but the threat of extra homework can stop bad behavior. The teacher can give extra homework to individual students, in the form of essays. Another form of extra homework, for an entire group, is announcing that there will be a quiz the next day over the material that they are supposed to be learning. This will often make the group pay more attention and behave better. Do not give students a quiz without giving them a chance to learn the material first. Extra homework is usually an individual punishment that serves as a model to the class, but on extreme occasions you can apply it to the whole group. **If you give extra homework as discipline, however, you must grade it.** Giving homework that you don't read is unethical.

3) FORCIBLE PRESSURE

If a child rebels and refuses to cooperate, you should remove the child from the group. If the child resists, you might use **forcible pressure** to make the child obey: carrying the child to the corner, forcing the stick from his/her hand, etc. Forcible pressure is not the same as corporal punishment. The intention of corporal punishment is to hurt the child. The objective of forcible pressure is to make the child cooperate. Forcible pressure makes the child get up and go where you tell him to, or let go of the object you demand from him. You might pick up and carry a small child to a seat away from the others. As soon as he cooperates, he will be comfortable. Still, if you use it at all, you should only use forcible pressure as a last resort.

4) INVOLVE THE SCHOOL AUTHORITIES. In extreme situations, you might want to expel students from the classroom or report them to the director or to their parents. However, these extreme techniques will only be effective if the director and the parents share the teacher's views on discipline. You may cause conflict with the students' parents or with your director. If possible, it is better to resolve the discipline problems in your classroom yourself.

STRATEGIES THAT YOU SHOULD NEVER USE

1) DO NOT LOWER GRADES FOR BAD BEHAVIOR. Using grades as a punishment confuses children, parents and teachers themselves: is there a learning problem or a discipline problem? Don't confuse successful learning with good behavior. A grade reflects how the student is doing academically. A punishment shows the child that his discipline is deficient. If you mix the two, you will confuse the student, the parents and your own assessment of his academic ability. You should grade the extra homework, and if the student doesn't do that homework, it will reflect on his grade, but you can't take off academic points just for poor discipline. **Behavior and academic progress are two separate things; don't confuse them.**

2) DO NOT USE A LOT OF CLASS TIME IN DISCIPLINE.
Disciplinary action should be short, so that the rest of the students can continue with their class. If the teacher spends too much time arguing or disciplining one student, the others become bored and distracted. They will stop learning and may behave badly, too. Often a student behaves badly because he really wants attention, even if it is negative attention. When you dedicate time to disciplining students, you give more attention to badly-behaved students, which may motivate them to behave badly more often. **So keep any interruptions for discipline**

to a minimum of time. When the child is behaving well again, welcome him back to the group, show him that you still like him and then continue with the activity.

3) NEVER RIDICULE, BELITTLE, REJECT OR INSULT STUDENTS. Never humiliate them, shout at them or make a public spectacle of them. Constant ridicule (emotional abuse) makes students afraid to take risks and to participate. If you destroy a student's self-esteem, you destroy his/her ability to learn.

4) NEVER GET ANGRY, RESENTFUL OR VINDICTIVE. The saying "Don't get mad; get even," means that you shouldn't lose your head or scream at the child. Take effective measures to control him, but never show that you are upset. Getting angry destroys your authority and your health, as well as reducing your students' ability to learn.

5) NEVER USE CORPORAL PUNISHMENT, RIDICULE, OR INSULTS.

Never hit, hurt or physically abuse students. Don't pull their hair, force them to kneel on bottle caps or make them stand for hours holding heavy books in their hands. You can go to jail for physical abuse, and your students can be permanently traumatized.

6) NEVER CONSIDER STUDENTS YOUR FRIENDS. You are their teacher; you have the authority and the responsibility to teach all your students and treat them equally, with no special preferences. The teacher-student relationship is not an equal relationship of friendship. A romantic or sexual relationship between a teacher and a student is totally unethical and unprofessional. This kind of relationship, called sexual abuse, is coercive because the teacher has the power to grade or fail the student.

PREVENTION OR DISCIPLINE?

PREVENTION IS PREFERABLE.

Ideally, you should manage the class with pacing, good emotional relations, and rewards. Discipline should not be necessary. Only use disciplinary techniques when prevention has failed. Still, you will probably have occasional problems, and the children need to know that you can control the group. They need to know what you will tolerate and what the limits are. However, concentrate on the positive aspects of group control.

WHAT IS THE PROPORTION OF PREVENTION OF PROBLEMS AND DISCIPLINE IN YOUR CLASSROOM?

Ideally, your control of the group should be 100% prevention of problems, 0% discipline. Realistically, you may use prevention 90% of the time and discipline 10%. But if you find yourself using 50% prevention and 50% discipline, or getting angry repeatedly, you have a problem. If you find that your groups are getting difficult consistently, and that you need to discipline them constantly, you need to reflect. You should examine your conscience and discover what you are doing wrong. Either you need to change your lesson plan or you need to change your attitude.

How are you planning your classes? Maybe your classes need to be more fun, more dynamic. If students are having fun, they will cooperate with you. Bored or unhappy students behave badly. Check your classes. A good class should be fun for students, as much as possible.

You also need to examine your attitude. Your relationship with students should be affectionate and playful, fun for both you and them. If you are a perfectionist, with impossibly high standards, you will have problems with your students. You need to be patient, understanding and tolerant of their failings. Most importantly, you need to have a real, sincere love for each student. This is an indispensable quality that teachers must have.

EFFECTIVENESS

What is your motivation for disciplining your students? Your basic reason for controlling your group should be to give effective classes and teach your students. You should not try to punish or hurt students who behave badly. "Revenge is sweet," they say, but it is not effective. Sometimes teachers may want to "give a student what he deserves." Rewarding a noisy class with dynamic, fun activities or expressing affection and admiration for a difficult student may seem unjust. However, justice is not the important thing. Effective prevention of problems is the important thing. Helping children learn and enjoy learning is the important thing.

FOR MORE INFORMATION,

See the following article online:

Magdalena Sulich's *"Keeping Discipline in the Classroom,"* published in *Forum Online Journal of English Teaching*, July 2004.

http://exchanges.state.gov/englishteaching/forum-journal.html

Professor Sulich stresses the importance of keeping control, that students really want discipline more than just friendliness. She also suggests that teachers should stand next to noisy students in order to control them better by the teacher's physical presence.

The following article, *Classroom Management Tips for Teachers*, by ESL Pro Systems, has useful advice.

Classroom Management Tips for Teachers:

by Patrick J. Selby, M.A.ESL Pro Systems www.esl-pro.com

Each week ESL Pro Systems presents informative articles and learning tips to our readers. This week we are focusing on classroom management tips for teachers of young ESL learners.

There are, of course, many different practices that are used for good classroom management. As with all classroom management practices, adapt what you like to your classroom, taking account the age, ethnicity, and personality of the class as a group, and of you as a teacher.

Maintaining good order in classrooms is one of the most difficult tasks facing young inexperienced teachers. The task has become more difficult over the past few decades as young people's attitudes to people in authority have changed dramatically. Some of the changes have led to greater self-confidence in students. Others-such as the acceptance of violence to achieve ends, attitudes to substance abuse and an increasing lack of respect for authority-have made classroom management and life in school generally more difficult, and more demanding, on those who are charged with maintaining a positive learning environment.

Many disruptive behaviors in the classroom can be alleviated before they become serious discipline problems. Such behaviors can be reduced by the teacher's ability to employ effective organizational practices. Such practices are at the heart of the teaching process and are essential to establishing and maintaining classroom control.

The following set of organizational practices should help to establish effective control of the classroom by the teacher:

1. Get off to a good start

The first "honeymoon" encounter between the

teacher and the students is when they formulate their impressions of the teacher. Students sit quietly, raise their hands to respond and are generally well behaved. The teacher is easily misled into thinking that this is an ideal class and may relax their vigilance. Students within a week will begin to test the waters to see what they can "get away with". It is during this period that the effective teacher will establish the expected ground-rules for classroom behavior.

2. Learn school policies

Prior to meeting the class for the first time, the teacher should become familiar with school policies concerning acceptable student behavior and disciplinary procedures. The teacher should definitely know what the school expects from both student and teacher in regard to discipline.

3. Establish rules

Establish a set of classroom rules to guide the behavior of students at once. Discuss the rationale of these rules with the students to ensure they understand and see the need for each rule. Keep the list of rules short. The rules most often involve paying attention, respect for others, excessive noise, securing materials and completion of homework assignments.

4. Be well prepared

"Overplan" the lessons for the first week or two. It is important for the teacher to impress on the students from the outset that he or she is organized and confident of their ability to get through the syllabus.

5. Learn names

Devise a seating arrangement whereby students' names are quickly learned. Calling a student by his or her name early in the year gives the student an increased sense of well being. It also gives a teacher greater control of situations. "Kyoko, stop talking and finish your work" is more effective than "Let us stop talking and finish our work".

6. Be firm and consistent

A teacher can be firm yet still be supportive and friendly with students. A firm teacher can provide an environment where the students feel safe and secure. Many teachers report that it is easier to begin the year in a firm manner and relax later, than

128

to begin in a lax manner and then try to become firm.

The following guidelines come from a teacher with 35 years of experience in primary school teaching.

Lupita's guidelines for Group Control

(Personal interview with G.G.U., October 2004)

Planning:

You get "presence" from experience and from being sure of what you are going to do. You need to have your lesson well planned, to know exactly what the limits of your tolerance are, and to know exactly what you will do if your students misbehave.

Consistency:

Never promise a reward or a punishment that you cannot give. You need to be congruent and fair. Calculate your possibilities of success before you give an order so that you won't lose authority. If a child refuses to obey, tell him that is fine, but that you will use the "law of ice"—ignoring him totally until he is ready to cooperate.

Authority:

Be a friendly teacher, but do not be just a friend. You are the organizer and the authority. You need to control the situation. Don't let the situation control you. Sometimes other teachers may try to take away your authority. Don't let them do it. Talk to them privately, or organize your class in a way that minimizes intervention from other teachers or directors. Do not ask the director for any help in disciplining students. (Lupita says that in 40 years of teaching, not one director has given any constructive help to her.)

Motivation:

Begin your class with something especially attractive to give students motivation to learn. Then they will learn better.

Students' Responsibility:

Give students responsibility for their own learning and for their own discipline. Have the students help you make rules for the class, and make those rules clear from the beginning. Give them as much freedom as possible.

Other sources of help:

Teachers of special classes (English, music) often have problems because the students aren't "their" group. Students become accustomed to one style or set of rules, and you need to impose a different one. Ask other teachers for their cooperation; explain what you need to them so there is consistency between teachers. Some parents are understanding and helpful, and you can use them for support, but don't rely on all parents to support you or enforce your rules.

Use Creativity:

If you have a problem because your students gossip when they sharpen their pencils, invent a strategy so you don't have to scold them constantly—have them attach plastic bags to the side of their desks for the pencil shavings.

Get to know your students:

See them as individual human beings, understand their needs. Use contracts to discipline them, or place them where they will work effectively. Involve students who are distracted or talking, keeping them too busy to talk.

Ignore problem students:

Use the "cold shoulder" (law of ice) with students who try to cause problems intentionally. Do not use forcible pressure.

Focus the group:

Use group physical activity or routines to concentrate students: Games are good.

Be sensitive:

First, do no harm. Be understanding and empathetic with each student, and be sensitive to the overall mood of the class. Constantly adjust your lesson to their feelings. *(G.G.U. 2004)*

CONCLUSION

Teachers need to keep a delicate balance: neither authoritarian nor ineffectual. You need to control the group and not permit the group to control you. At the same time, your control of the group helps the students learn together happily and effectively. Good class planning, with a balance of active and quiet activities, pacing the activities to change often, especially if the class is beginning to get bored, and using body language, tone of voice and physical proximity to show your affection for children, should prevent most problems and reduce the necessity for discipline.

EXERCISE IN GROUP CONTROL

In the following situations, teachers' mistakes cause problems in group control. What mistake did the teachers made in each case, and what should the teachers have done?

Example: A 2nd grader gets out a toy and plays noisily while the teacher is trying to explain the material. The teacher hits the child.

Answer: <u>Hitting the child was a mistake because teachers shouldn't use corporal punishment. The teacher should have organized a fun, competitive game about the material. This way other students would pressure the badly behaved child to pay attention. The student would feel motivated.</u>

1. Last Friday, the teacher promised to play a favorite game with the 3rd graders if they worked well. They worked well but there wasn't enough time for the game. Today they are very difficult. The teacher threatens to send the whole group to the principal's office, but he/she knows that this is impossible.

2. One of the kindergarteners has a temper tantrum. The teacher spends 15 minutes trying to calm the child down. Meanwhile, other children get restless. The teacher loses control of the class.

3. The 6th graders are very difficult this week. They don't like the activities, the homework or their grades. They even invent a nickname for the teacher. The teacher screams, "You little monsters! Maybe your parents let you insult them, but I can't stand you!"

4. The kindergarten class is very restless after 20 minutes of circling pictures of basic verbs, so the teacher gives them an exercise where they color pictures of verbs. The students are still very restless, they don't want to work and they are getting out of control.

5. Three of the 4th graders finished the activity very fast. Now they are playing and throwing paper. The teacher tells them that he/she will take 3 points off their grades as punishment.

6. Two 6th graders are talking. The teacher ignores them. They begin to talk more loudly, and other students enter the conversation. Soon, the whole class is talking, and the teacher cannot control them.

UNIT 5: DRAWINGS, SONGS, GAMES AND STORIES

INTRODUCTION

New teachers can feel as if they are in a war with no weapons. "How can I ever motivate these kids? They interrupt and scream constantly! Do I have to use boring drills and workbook pages to keep them focused? Help!" Teachers need tools to motivate students, keep discipline, and make learning more fun. This last section contains tools for teachers to use with students.

DRAWINGS

Drawing is a very useful talent for teaching. Even if you are not a great artist, knowing how to communicate concepts by simple pictures will help you immensely. Some tips on how to draw follow.

| Happy | Sad | Excited | Scared | Tired |

| Sick | Angry | Disgusted | Puzzled | Provocative |

To draw facial expressions, observe the size and shape of the eyes, the angle of the eyebrows and the mouth, and the symmetry of the face. The shape of the face itself can be a simple circle.

Stand   Walk   Jump   Dance   Run

Look For   Swim   Fall Asleep   Shiver   Show Off

When you draw movement or corporal positions, observe the lines and angles of the spine, head, shoulders, hips and feet. Add facial expression to give the picture more emotional impact.

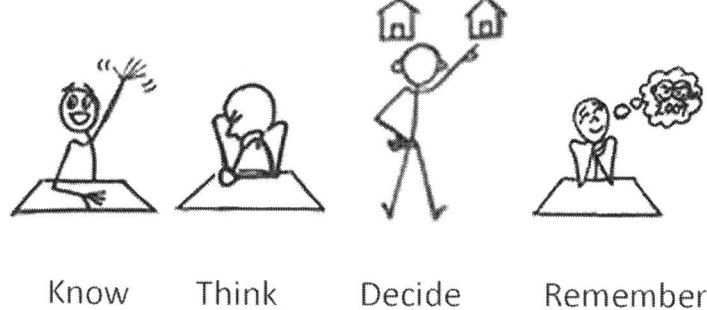

Know   Think   Decide   Remember

Translate "invisible" words into expressive actions. Children raise their hand in class when they <u>know</u> the answer. We often rest our head on our hand when we think. When we decide, we choose one of two or more possible options. The picture for <u>remember</u> uses a cartoon technique: the thought bubble showing two happy faces and a date in the past.

Bring/Take   Lend/Borrow   Lose/Find

It is easier to illustrate concepts using pairs of antonyms (opposites) or related words. We <u>bring</u> something here, but we <u>take</u> something away to another place. To <u>lend</u> is to give something temporarily; to <u>borrow</u> is to receive. When we <u>lose</u> something, it is gone, but when we <u>find</u> something, we feel happy.

DRAWINGS AS REWARDS

Drawings serve multiple purposes. Comical "monster" drawings serve as rewards for children, motivating them to work and learn. Teachers can photocopy pages of monsters and cut them into cards. Some concepts are easy for students to visualize and for teachers to capture in "monster cards." Simple nouns for classroom objects or for clothing, adjectives, colors and action verbs make good cards. The cards work as a memory aid for the students, as well as helping the teacher keep control of the group.

Students who finish a task, bring their homework or open their books to the correct page get a card. The children can color the card, stick it on a notebook, trade it with a friend or collect it. Unlike grades, monster cards are an immediate reward. When the students collect a certain number of cards, they can also exchange the cards for a bigger poster.

Drawings as Didactic Tools

As well as helping teachers keep order in the classroom, the "monster cards" and other drawings illustrate English vocabulary in a memorable way. The "ABC monsters" on the next page help students remember the pronunciation of English letters. "A" looks like a cowboy who says, "¡Ey, nena!" "E" is smiling, because it is necessary to smile when you pronounce that letter. "I" is shouting "¡Ay!" because its head or point is cut off. "O" has a round mouth that says "o." The two ends of "U" point at each other, because the letter is pronounced like "you." "B" has its mouth firmly closed, while "V" is making a rabbit face, its teeth visible. "G" smiles because it contains the "E" sound, while "J" holds its fist in the air and shouts, "Yay!" Each picture serves as a memory aid that explains the pronunciation of the letter.

Teachers may use "monster cards" to help students visualize more abstract concepts such as the use of the auxiliaries "do/does," the days of the week, prepositions, personal pronouns, question words, adverbs of frequency, etc.

A monster B monster C monster D monster

E monster F monster G monster

H monster i monster J monster K monster

L monster M monster N monster

O monster   P monster

Q monster   R monster   S monster

T monster   U monster   V monster

W monster   X monster   Y monster   Z monster

Do? monsters   Yes, do monsters

Does? monster   Yes, does monsters

Yes, I do.
No, I don't.   monster

don't monsters   doesn't monster

146

in monster   on monster

next to monsters   under monster

in front of monster   behind monster

to monster

Where? Monster

Who? Monster

What color? Monster

When? Monster

never monster

LARGE POSTERS

Large pictures or posters also make excellent prizes for good grades. Larger pictures make it easier for students to understand concepts such as the weather or the seasons of the year with their months. They can teach related words regarding vacations or a particular holiday. Valentine's Day pictures and cards for students to fill out also help students' self-esteem and social skills. 5th and 6th graders are often interested in mythology, and they will enjoy pictures of ancient gods and goddesses. Ecology is another favorite theme for 5th and 6th graders. Encourage these students to design their own "monster" posters about pollution.

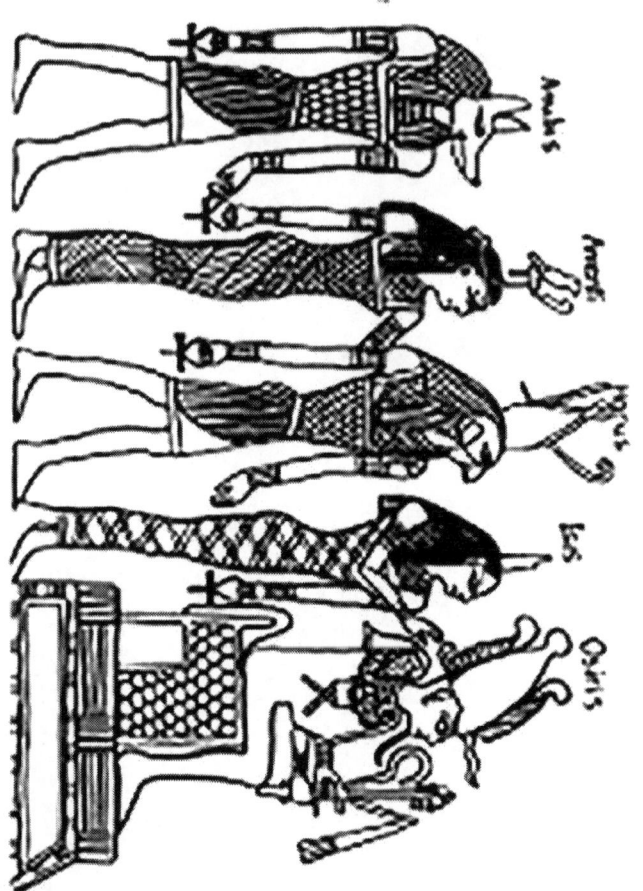

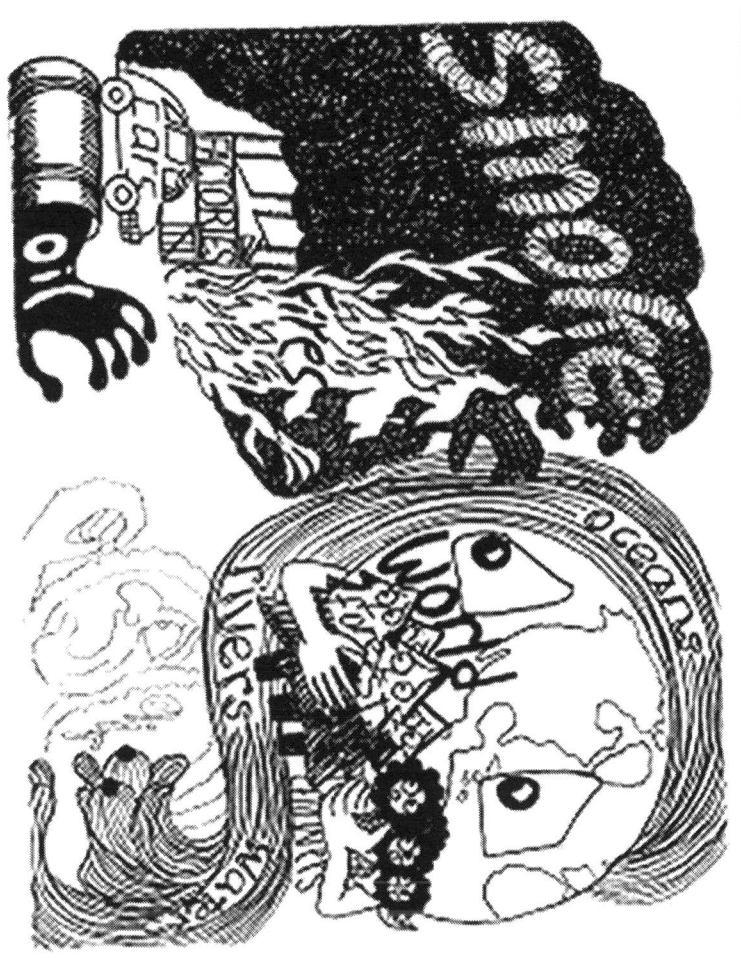

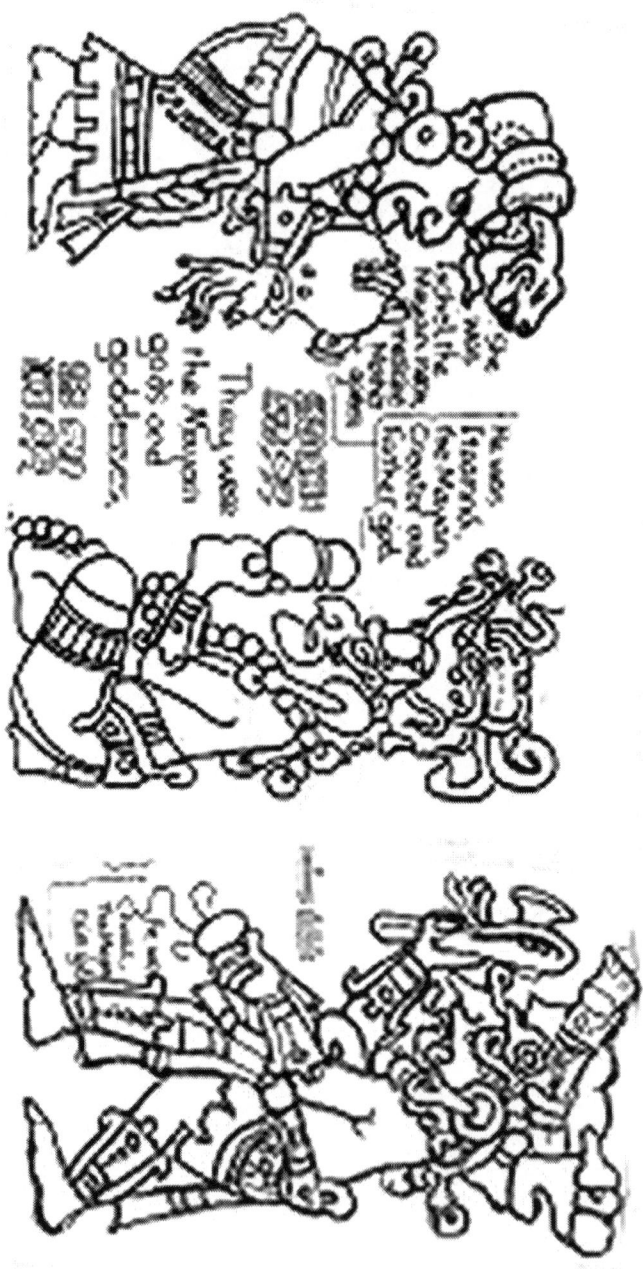

Puzzles, hidden pictures, mazes, etc. are didactic. They teach vocabulary as well as giving the fastest students a fun extra activity to do while the slower students are still finishing the exam or workbook page.

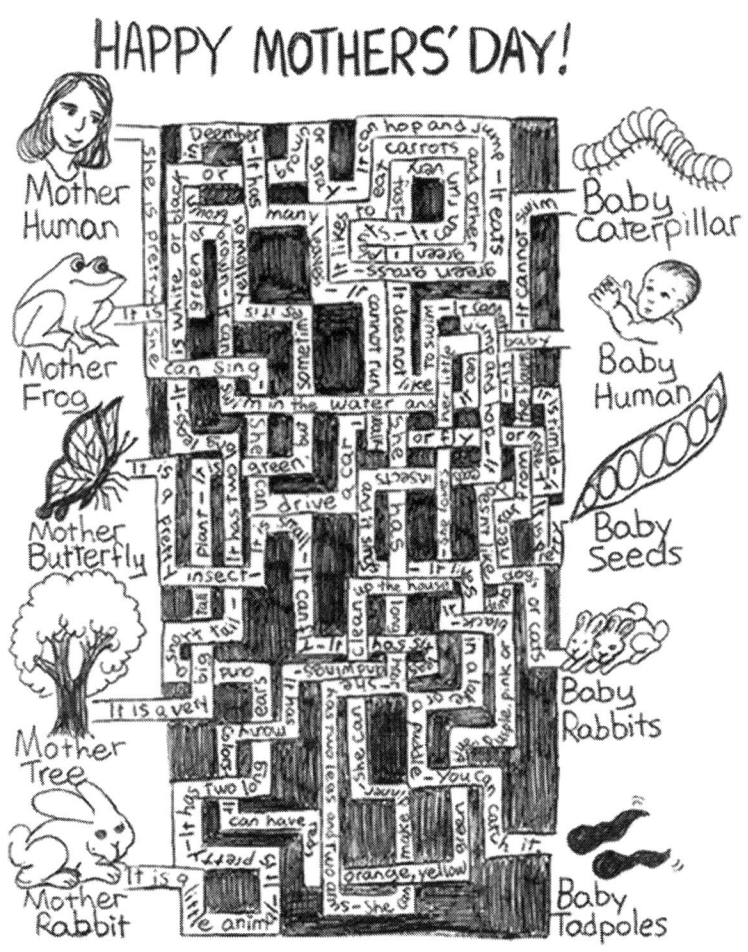

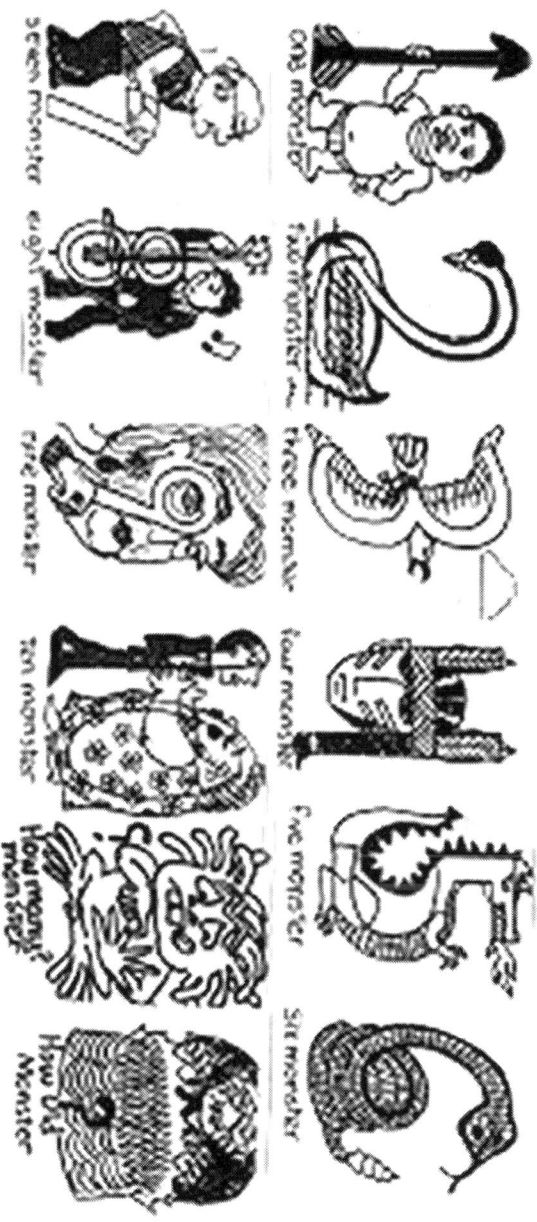

161

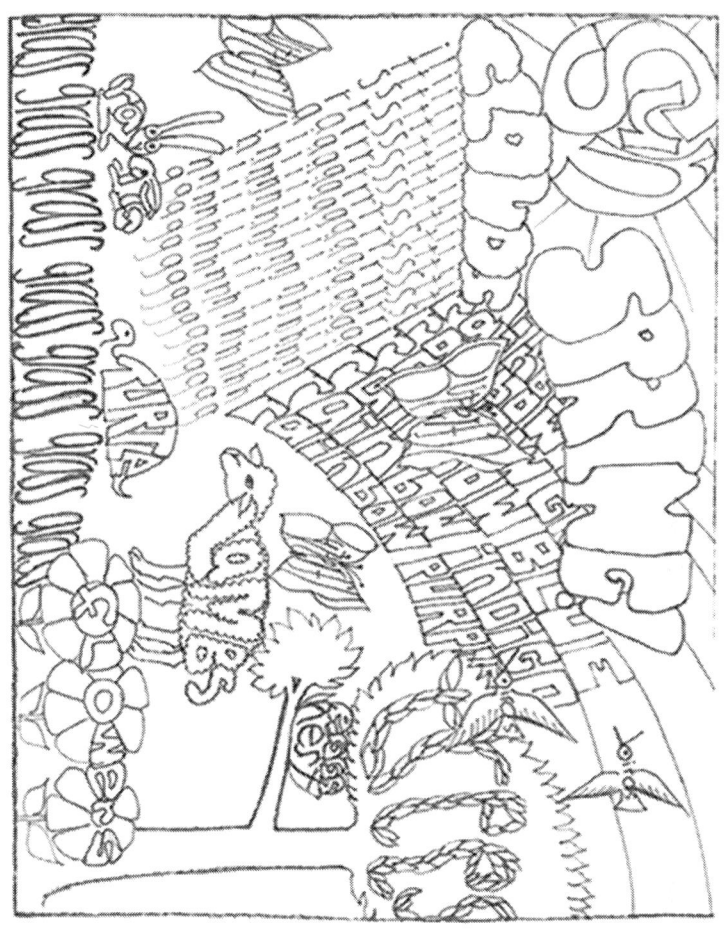

SONGS FOR KINDERGARTEN AND EARLY ELEMENTARY SCHOOL

Teachers can use songs, especially funny songs, singing games or songs with hand movements, to introduce new vocabulary or structures. They are also a fun way for children to practice what they have learned. Most of the songs below appear on YouTube or in children's music CDs. (See list at the end of this unit.) You can learn more songs from other English speakers, invent your own words or melodies, or adapt existing songs to fit your needs. If you can't sing, use the songs as chants or spoken rhymes. Use hand movements as much as possible to help children understand the words and to involve kinesthetic children.

QUESTION SONG: FOR DELIA (C-G7-F-G7-C)

1) What, what, what is it? –It's a nut, It's a cutter, it's a door that's shut.

2) Where, where, where is it? –Here or there, At my house, near Tuxtla or on the chair.

3) When, when, when is it? –Now or then, April seventh at half past ten.

4) Who, who, who is it? –It is Sue, It is Lucas or it is you.

5) How much, how much? –Not too much; A meter, a liter, twenty pesos for lunch.

6) How many, how many? –Not too many, Two, three, four, five, ten or twenty.

7) Whose, whose, whose is it? –Marilu's, It's yours, it's mine, it's Dr. Fu Manchu's.

7) How, how, how is it? –It's fine now, It's hot, it's cold, it is quiet, it's loud.

8) Why, why, why is it?—So I can buy it, Because I like it or just to try it.

9) How long, how long?—All day long, Just a minute, till I finish this song.

<u>THE LITTLE SKUNK'S HOLE</u> (Tune: Turkey in the Straw. G, D7, C, Em, D7, G)

Oh, I put my head down a little skunk's hole, And the little skunk said, "Well, bless my soul,

Take it out, take it out, take it out, remove it."

Well, I didn't take it out, so the little skunk said, "If you don't take it out, you'll wish you had,

Take it out, take it out, take it out!" Pee-yew! I removed it!

<u>HAPPY BIRTHDAY TO YOU</u> (G, D7, C, G)

Happy birthday to you, happy birthday to you,

Happy birthday, dear *Susie,* Happy birthday to you.

(Happy birthday to you, you belong in a zoo,

You look like a monkey, and you smell like one, too.

Happy birthday to you, Fried tomatoes and stew,

You look like a gorilla, And your mother does, too.)

G<small>OOD</small> M<small>ORNING</small> T<small>O</small> Y<small>OU</small> (C, G7, F, C)

Good morning to you! Good morning to you!

We're all in our places with sunshiny faces,

Oh, this is the way to start a new day.

T<small>HE</small> A<small>LPHABET</small> S<small>ONG</small>   (CCFC/ FCG7C/ CFCG7/ CFCG7 /CCFC /FCG7C)

(Tune: "Twinkle, Twinkle, Little Star")

A B C D E F G, H I J K LMNOP, Q R S, T U V, W, X Y Z,

Oh, how happy we shall be,

When we learn our ABC.

TEN GREEN SPOTTED FROGS (C, Am, G7, C)

Ten green spotted frogs, sat on a spotted log,

Eating some most delicious bugs. Yum! Yum!

One jumped into the pool, where it was nice and cool.

Then there were nine green spotted frogs.

(Nine green spotted frogs, etc.)

THIS IS THE WAY THE DOCTOR WORKS (D, A7, D) (Tune: "The Mulberry Bush")

This is the way the doctor works, the doctor works, the doctor works,

This is the way the doctor works, So early in the morning.

(Farmer, Nurse, Teacher, Driver, etc. Mime the work each person does.)

Today Is Monday (Chords: E, B7, E)

Today is Monday, Today is Monday,

Monday: Flag Day, Monday: Flag Day, The first day of the week.

Today is Tuesday (x2) Tuesday: Domino's (x2) the second day of the week.

Today is Wednesday (x2) Wednesday: Movies (x2) the third day of the week.

Today is Thursday (x2) Thursday: Salsa (x2) the fourth day of the week.

Today is Friday (x2) Friday: Weekend (x2) the fifth day of the week.

Today is Saturday (x2) Saturday: Play (x2) the sixth day of the week.

Today is Sunday (x2) Sunday: Family (x2) the seventh day of the week.

(Mime special activities, such as saluting the flag, etc. or special school subjects studied on specific days, for example: Sports, Music, Religion, Computer, Drawing, etc..)

HE'S GOT THE WHOLE WORLD IN HIS HANDS (C, G7, C)

He's got the whole world in his hands (X3) He's got the whole world in his hands.

He's got you and me in his hands (X3) He's got the whole world in his hands.

He's got the father and the mother in his hands (X3) He's got the whole world in his hands.

He's got the sister and the brother in his hands (X3) He's got the whole world in his hands.

He's got the little tiny baby in his hands (X3) He's got the whole world in his hands.

He's got grandmother and grandfather in his hands (X3) He's got the whole world...etc.

He's got me and my friend in his hands (X3) He's got the whole world in his hands.

(Children mime the words, making a big circle for "the whole world," pointing to the teacher and to themselves for "you and me," miming a moustache for father, earrings for mother, ponytails for sister, hair sticking up for brother, rocking a baby for baby, holding a cane for grandfather and grandmother, and putting an arm around "me and my friend.")

CAN YOU SWIM? (G, D7, G)

Can you <u>swim</u>? Can you <u>swim</u>? No, I cannot. Yes, I can. (X3)

Can you <u>swim</u>? Can you <u>swim</u>? Yes, I can!

(fly/ walk/ run/ jump/ sit/ sleep/ ride/ come/ go/ eat/ drink/ dance, etc.)

(Children mime the actions. For "No, I cannot," they shrug their shoulders and shake their heads. For "Yes, I can," they show their arm muscles like champions.)

ARE YOU SLEEPING? (E, A, E)

Are you <u>sleeping,</u> are you <u>sleeping,</u> Little John? Little John?

No, I am not <u>sleeping,</u> I am doing homework, Yes, I am. Yes, I am.

(Are   you fishing/swimming/drawing/eating/drinking/driving, etc.?)

(Children mime the actions, make a "no" sign waving their fingers in front of them, and miming writing for "I am

doing homework." Fold arms and nod head for "Yes, I am.")

FINGER SONG (D, A7, D)

Where is <u>Thumbkin,</u> where is <u>Thumbkin?</u> Here I am! Here I am!

How are you today, sir? I am fine, thank you. Run away! Run away!

(Pointer...Tall man...Ring man....Pinky)

(Put hand over eyes and look around for "Where is Thumbkin?" Bring right hand with thumb up in front of face for "Here I am!" Pretend to talk to thumb for "How are you today, sir?" Move thumb for "I am fine, thank you." Put right hand behind back for "Run away!" Repeat with 2nd, 3rd, 4th and 5th fingers.)

THE ANTS GO MARCHING

(Em C G7 G7/ Em C G7 G7/ Em Am Em B7/ B7 B7/ Am Em Am Em)

The ants go marching one by one, hurrah! Hurrah! (x2)

The ants go marching one by one, the last one stops to suck his thumb

*And the ants go marching, all around and under the ground

And through the drain and out in the rain.

The ants go marching two by two....The last one stops to tie his shoe.*

The ants go marching three by three...The last one stops to climb a tree.*

The ants go marching four by four...The last one stops to shut the door.*

The ants go marching five by five....The last one stops to take a dive.*

The ants go marching six by six....The last one stops to pick up sticks.*

The ants go marching seven by seven…The last one stops to go to Heaven.*

The ants go marching eight by eight…The last one stops to climb a gate.*

The ants go marching nine by nine….The last one stops to check the time*.

The ants go marching ten by ten…The last one stops to shout, "The end!"

(Hold up fingers to show numbers. Mime actions. Draw a circle with finger in the air for "all around," finger goes down for "under the ground," then over for "through the drain," and up again for "out in the rain.")

APPLES AND BANANAS (G D7 G)

I like, I like, I like apples and bananas, I like, I like, I like apples and bananas.

I do not like, like, like vinegar and onions, I do not like, like, like, vinegar and onions.

(You like / he likes / she likes / we like / they like)

(Rub stomachs and look appreciative for "I like." Mime eating an apple and peeling a banana. Wave fingers in a negative gesture for "I do not like." Pinch nose for "vinegar and onions." Point to different people for the different personal pronouns.)

Color Song (E, B7, E)

Red is an apple, orange is an orange, yellow is the yellow sun in the sky,

Green is the green grass, blue is the blue sky, purple is a flower that grows so high.

Pink is a pink pig, brown's a cup of coffee,

White are your tennis shoes and your school shirt.

Black are your school shoes, and black is Batman,

Grey are your school pants and your school skirt.

(Children mime objects as they sing)

THE EENSIE-WEENSIE SPIDER (E, B7, E)

The eensie-weensie spider went up the garden spout,

Down came the rain and washed the spider out.

Along came the sun and dried up all the rain,

And the eensie-weensie spider went up the spout again.

(Mime a spider going up the spout. Bring hands down for the rain, then pull hands to the left for "washed the spider out." Make a circle with both hands above head for the sun, pull hands up for "dried up all the rain," and mime the spider again at the end.)

HENRY, MY SON (D G D A7/ D- G- / D G DA7D)

Where did you go all day, Henry, my son? Where did you go all day, my handsome one?

To the woods, Mother, To the woods, Mother,

*Mother, come quick, I'm about to be sick, Gonna lay me down and die.

Who did you see there, Henry, my son? Who did you see there, my handsome one?

My sweetheart, Mother, my sweetheart, Mother, *

Mother, come quick...

What did you do there, Henry, my son? What did you do there, my handsome one?

We ate, Mother, we ate, Mother, * ***Mother, come quick...***

What did you eat there, Henry, my son? What did you eat there, my handsome one?

Eels, Mother, eels, Mother, * ***Mother, come quick...***

What color were they, Henry, my son? What color were they, my handsome one?

Green and yellow, Green and yellow, * ***Mother, come quick...***

Those weren't eels, Henry, my son! Those were snakes, my handsome one!

Yuck! Mother, Yuck! Mother, * ***Mother, come quick...***

(Children mime questions and answers. Gesture to call mother, hands on stomach for "I'm about to be sick," and back of hand on forehead for "Gonna lay me down and die.")

Old McDonald Had a Farm (G, D7, G)

Old McDonald had a farm, ee-I-ee-I-oh, And on that farm he had a cow, ee-I-ee-I-oh.

With a "moo, moo" here and a "moo, moo" there,

Here a "moo," there a "moo," everywhere a "moo, moo,"

Old McDonald had a farm, ee-I-ee-I-oh.

(horse / pig / sheep / dog / cat / duck / hen)

(Children mime the different animals: making horns for the cow, stamping for the horse, etc.)

Ten Little Indians (E, B7, E)

One little, two little, three little Indians, Four little, five little, six little Indians,

Seven little, eight little, nine little Indians, Ten little Indian boys.

Ten little, nine little, eight little Indians, seven little, six little, five little Indians,

Four little, three little, two little Indians, one little Indian boy.

(Children hold up fingers to indicate numbers.)

SHE WADED IN THE WATER (Tune: "John Brown's Body" G, C, D7, G)

She waded in the water and she got her <u>toes</u> all wet (x3),

but she didn't get her * * wet, yet.

(* = clap, clap.)* <u>Feet</u>, <u>ankles</u>, <u>calves</u>, <u>knees</u>, <u>thighs</u>

She waded in the water and she finally got it wet (x3), She finally got her bathing suit wet!

OH, DO YOU KNOW THE MUFFIN MAN? (G, D7, G)

Oh, do you know the <u>muffin man,</u> the <u>muffin man,</u> the <u>muffin man</u>?

Oh, do you know the <u>muffin man</u> that lives on Drury Lane?

Oh yes, I know the <u>muffin man</u>, the <u>muffin man</u>, the <u>muffin man,</u>

Oh yes, I know the <u>muffin man</u> that lives on Drury Lane.

(Children mime ringing a bell to represent the muffin man. Then they mime other jobs: <u>garbage man</u>, <u>water man</u>, <u>Gas Com man</u>, <u>knife sharpener</u>, <u>street cleaner</u>, <u>fruit seller</u>, shoeshine boy, etc)

JOHN BROWN'S BABY (Tune: John Brown's Body, G, C, D7, G)

John Brown's baby had a cold upon its chest (x2)

John Brown's baby had a cold upon its chest and they rubbed it with camphorated oil.

(In each verse, eliminate one more word and replace it with a gesture: "baby" is rocking a baby, "cold" is blowing the nose, "chest" is hitting the chest, and "camphorated oil" is pinching the nose shut.)

BINGO (G, D7, C, Em, D7, G)

There was a farmer had a dog and Bingo was its name, oh,

B-I-N-G-O, B-I-N-G-O, B-I-N-G-O and Bingo was its name, oh.

(In each verse, eliminate one letter and replace it with a clap)

SINGING CIRCLE GAMES

For all of these games, children form a circle and sing as they play the game.

SUSY IS WEARING A RED SKIRT (D, A7, D)

Susy is wearing a red skirt, red skirt, red skirt, Susy is wearing a red skirt, All day long.

Susy is wearing white socks, white socks, white socks,

Susy is wearing white socks, All day long.

(One child stands at the front of the room or in the middle of the circle and points to each piece of clothing as the rest of the children sing. Use the children's names instead of "Susy.")

HEAD, SHOULDERS, KNEES AND TOES (C G7 C C/C G7 G7 G7/ C G7 F F/G7 G7 C C)

Head, shoulders, knees and toes, knees and toes, (X2)

And eyes and ears and mouth and nose,

Head, shoulders, knees and toes, knees and toes.

(Children touch body parts mentioned in the song. Sing faster and faster.)

BLUEBIRD, BLUEBIRD (C G7 C)

Bluebird, bluebird, through my window, Bluebird, bluebird, through my window,

Bluebird, bluebird, through my window, Oh, Johnny, I am tired.

(Children form a circle, holding hands. One child, the "Bluebird," runs in and out of the circle going under the other children's hands. When the song finishes, the child touches the nearest classmate. That classmate becomes the new "Bluebird," while the old "Bluebird" joins the circle, holding hands with 2 classmates. You can vary the song according to the colors of the children's clothes: "Pink bird," "White bird," etc.)

<u>Did You Ever See A Laddie?</u>   (E, B7, E) (Laddie=boy. Lassie=girl)

Did you ever see a <u>laddie,</u> see a <u>laddie</u>, see a <u>laddie</u>, see a <u>laddie,</u>

Did you ever see a <u>laddie</u> go this way and that?

Go this way and that way and this way and that way,

Did you ever see a <u>laddie</u> go this way and that?

(Children form a circle. One child stands in the middle and invents a movement. The other children imitate it as they sing. If the child in the middle is a boy, they sing "Laddie," but if the child is a girl, they sing "Lassie." At the end of the verse, the child in the middle chooses another child to go in the middle, and the first child goes back into the circle.)

LONDON BRIDGE (D A7 D)

London Bridge is falling down, falling down, falling down,

London Bridge is falling down, my fair lady.

Build it up with silver and gold, silver and gold, silver and gold,

Build it up with silver and gold, my fair lady.

Silver and gold get stolen away, stolen away, stolen away,

Silver and gold get stolen away, my fair lady.

(Iron bars will rust and break / Sticks and stones will tumble and fall

/ Wood and clay get washed away.)

(Play this circle game like "A La Vibora, Vibora de la Mar." 2 children join hands to make a bridge. One child is "Silver" and the other is "Gold." The other children run under the bridge, holding each other by the waist. At the end of each verse, the "bridge" falls, capturing a child. That child must choose, "Silver or gold?" then go stand behind one of the "bridge" children. When all the children are captured, the "Silver" and "Gold" children pull on a rope to see which team is stronger.)

Hokey-Pokey (G, C, D7, G)

You put your <u>right hand</u> in, you take your <u>right hand</u> out,

You put your <u>right hand</u> in and you shake it all about,

You do the Hokey-Pokey and you turn yourself around,

That's what it's all about. Hey!

(Right/left: hand, foot, arm, leg, shoulder, hip. Head, butt, whole self)

(Children form a circle. They put the body part mentioned in the song into the center, then pull it out. They dance around in a circle for "You do the hokey-pokey and you turn yourself around," then jump up and shout for the "Hey!")

CHRISTMAS CAROLS

Having your group sing Christmas carols (songs) at a December school festival will show administrators, colleagues, parents and the students themselves how much English they have learned. It is a fun activity that will make you and your students proud.

Many of the songs below have Spanish equivalents, which makes it easy for Spanish-speaking students to learn the melodies and the meaning. Other Christmas carols are included because the words are repetitious and easy to learn. You can hear the melodies on YouTube (see the YouTube bibliography at the end of this unit) or on Christmas CDs. Guitar chords are marked as well.

THE WASSAIL SONG (D, Bm, D, D7 / G, D, Em, A// D GD, D GD/ G, A, Bm G/ D GA D)

Here we come a-wassailing among the leaves so green,

And here we come a-wandering, so fair to be seen,

 *Love and joy come to you, and to you your wassail, too

 And God bless you and send you a happy New Year,

And God send you a happy New Year.

We are not daily beggars that beg from door to door,

But we are neighbors' children whom you have seen before

*Love and joy come to you...

God bless the mistress of this house, God bless the master, too,

And all the little children that 'round the table go

*Love and joy come to you...

SILENT NIGHT *(Noche de Paz)* (A, A, E, A/ D A D A/ E F#m A/ A E A)

Silent night, holy night, all is calm, all is bright

Round yon Virgin, Mother and Child, Holy Infant so tender and mild,

Sleep in heavenly peace, sleep in heavenly peace.

Silent night, holy night, shepherds quake at the sight,

Glories stream from heaven afar, heavenly hosts sing, "Alleluia!"

Christ the Savior is born, Christ the Savior is born.

THE LITTLE DRUMMER BOY *(El Niño del Tambor)*

(D A7D/ D A7D/ G A7/ D G, D, A7/ D A7D/ G D)

Come, they told me *(pa-rumpum pum pum)* A newborn King to see *(pa-rum..)*

Our finest gifts we bring *(pa-rum..)* To lay before the King *(pa-rum.. x3)*

So to honor him *(pa-rum..)* When we come.

Baby Jesus *(pa-rum..)* I am a poor boy too *(pa-rum..)*

I have no gift to bring *(pa-rum..)* That's fit to give a King *(pa-rum.. x3)*

Shall I play for you *(pa-rum..)* On my drum?

Mary nodded *(pa-rum..)* The ox and lamb kept time *(pa-rum..)*

I played my drum for Him *(pa-rum..)* I played my best for him *(pa-rum.. x3)*

Then He smiled at me *(pa-rum..)* Me and my drum.

WE WISH YOU A MERRY CHRISTMAS (G, D7, C, G)

We wish you a merry Christmas, (x3) and a Happy New Year.

Glad tidings we bring, to you and your kin,

Glad tidings for Christmas and a Happy New Year.

Oh bring us a figgy pudding (x3) and bring it right here.

We won't go until we get some (x3) so bring it right here.

192

ANGELS WE HAVE HEARD ON HIGH *(Gloria de los Angeles)* (E, B7, A, E)

Angels we have heard on high, sweetly singing o'er the plains

And the mountains in reply, echoing their joyous strains.

Gloria in excelsis Deo (X2)

Shepherds, why this jubilee? Why these songs of happy cheer?

What great brightness did you see? What glad tidings did you hear?

Gloria in excelsis Deo (X2)

Come to Bethlehem and see him whose birth the angels sing

Come adore on bended knee Christ the Lord, the newborn King.

Gloria in excelsis Deo (X2)

THE TWELVE DAYS OF CHRISTMAS (E B7 A E—E F# E)

On the first day of Christmas, my true love sent to me: a partridge in a pear tree.

On the second day of Christmas, my true love sent to me:

2 turtle doves and a partridge in a pear tree.

On the third day of Christmas, my true love sent to me:

3 French hens, 2 turtle doves, and a partridge in a pear tree.

On the fourth day of Christmas, my true love sent to me:

4 calling birds, 3 French hens, 2 turtle doves and a partridge in a pear tree.

On the fifth day of Christmas, my true love sent to me:

5 gold rings! 4 calling birds, 3 French hens, 2 turtle doves and a partridge...

On the sixth day of Christmas, my true love sent to me:

6 geese a-laying, 5 gold rings! 4 calling birds, 3 French hens, 2 turtledoves...

On the seventh day of Christmas, my true love sent to me:

7 swans a-swimming, 6 geese a-laying, 5 gold rings! 4 calling birds, 3 French hens...

On the eighth day of Christmas, my true love sent to me:

8 maids a-milking, 7 swans a-swimming, 6 geese a-laying, 5 gold rings! 4 calling birds...

On the ninth day of Christmas, my true love sent to me:

9 ladies dancing, 8 maids a-milking, 7 swans a-swimming, 6 geese a-laying...

On the tenth day of Christmas, my true love sent to me:

10 lords a-leaping, 9 ladies dancing, 8 maids a-milking, 7 swans a-swimming...

On the 'leventh day of Christmas, my true love sent to me:

11 pipers piping, 10 lords a-leaping, 9 ladies dancing, 8 maids a-milking...

On the twelfth day of Christmas, my true love sent to me:

12 drummers drumming, 11 pipers piping, 10 lords a-leaping, 9 ladies dancing...

RHYMES AND GAMES

Rhymes, finger games and other games are another fun way for students to get the drill practice that they need. You can use rhymes and finger games to collect and focus a group that is getting out of control. Active games are especially good for kindergarteners and young, kinesthetic children. These activities make good introductions to new vocabulary and structures, or a fun way to practice the new English the students have learned. They can serve as a stimulus or a reward at the end of a class, too. Learn the rules of other games from English speakers and learners, find them on the Internet, or invent your own.

FINGER GAMES

Here is the church and here is the steeple. Open the doors—Where are all the people?

Here is the church and here is the steeple. Open the doors—Here are all the people!

Here are mother's knives and forks, Here's father's table,

Here's sister's looking glass, Here's baby's cradle.

Rhymes and Jump-Rope Chants

One, two, buckle my shoe, three, four, shut the door,

Five, six, pick up sticks, Seven, eight, Lay them straight,

Nine, ten, a big fat hen.

('Leven, twelve, dig and delve,

Thirteen, fourteen, maids a-courting, Fifteen, sixteen, maids a-kissing,

Seventeen, eighteen, maids a-waiting, Nineteen, twenty, my plate's empty.)

Two, four, six, eight, Who do we appreciate? Fulano!

Solomon Grundy, Born on Monday, Christened on Tuesday, Married on Wednesday,

Sick on Thursday, Worse on Friday, Died on Saturday, Buried on Sunday,

And that is the tale of Solomon Grundy.

Cinderella dressed in yellow, Went upstairs to kiss her fellow,

Made a mistake, kissed a snake, How many doctors did it take? One, two, three...

Pepe and Mary sitting in a tree, K-I-S-S-I-N-G,

First comes love, then comes marriage, Then comes the baby in the baby carriage.

Charlie Chaplin went to France, to teach the ladies how to dance,

A heel, a toe, around we go, a heel, a toe, around we go,

Bow to the captain, curtsey to the Queen, touch the bottom of the submarine.

You can invent your own chants and rhymes to help students learn difficult concepts, grammar and spelling. The following chants are didactic rhymes for teaching English.

+ Irregular Past Participles with –N (The Crazy Pilot Rhyme)

He's been to the city, he's taken a train,

He's gone to the airport, he's stolen a plane,

He's driven it out, taken off, up he's flown,

He's forgotten that he's just a kid, not yet grown.

They've written instructions the boy hasn't seen,

He's broken the motor, there's no gasoline,

He's given up hope, fallen down; Death has won,

The buzzards have eaten him. My story's done.

+ Pronunciation of –ED past tense

For verbs that end in D or T, you add a syllable: say the E.

Verb doesn't end in D or T? Then don't pronounce the letter "E."

(Planted, landed, loaded: 2 syllables. Stopped, knocked, breathed: 1 syllable)

CLASSIC SPELLING RULE

"I" before "E," except after "C," or when sounded like "A" as in "neighbor" and "weigh."

DO-IT-YOURSELF DIDACTIC MATERIALS

Most young children are kinesthetic learners. Touching objects helps them learn. Collect attractive toys, puppets, models and miniature objects to use in class. You can make your own miniatures with a cutter, a roll of packing tape, scraps of cloth, some old boxes and recycled plastic containers. Cut up old plastic bottles and containers then tape them together to create tiny furniture, houses and cars. Matchboxes taped together make a chest of drawers or bureau. Add a mirror made from the shiny side of a potato chip bag, framed in cardboard and taped onto the chest of drawers. A rectangular plastic bottle or cardboard box makes a good refrigerator, cupboard, bed or table. You can fill the cupboard with miniature cereal boxes, bags of rice, cans of tuna fish, etc, making small cardboard models and taping pictures from a supermarket advertisement onto them. Round bottles make small living room tables or chairs: use a cutter to make a seat from the bottom of the bottle, leaving four legs at equal distances. Cut another bottle to make the back of the chair then tape the two parts together. Plastic bottle caps make good bowls (and good counters for board games); discs of plastic cut from a container are little plates and toothpaste caps make small glasses. You can cut the top of a yogurt bottle to make a toilet. Create the toilet seat and the lid from more yogurt bottles. Attach them by cutting a little hole in one end of each piece and tying them together with dental floss. Use extra pieces of cloth to make little curtains, sheets, blankets and towels, and put these things into shoe boxes, painted to look like rooms. Vocabulary for houses, rooms and furniture will be much clearer if students can actually see and touch small models of the objects.

For role-plays and theatrical productions, make your own puppets, masks, costumes and props (objects used in theaters) from recycled objects. Cut out the middle of a plastic bottle, then tape the two ends together to make the cylindrical head of a puppet. Cover this head with cloth or "fomi" (craft foam), using yarn for hair and drawing the features with permanent markers. You can sustain the puppet by putting your middle finger through the mouth of the bottle. Then sew the body from cloth and attach it to the head. Old socks or gloves can be the base for good puppets, too. Stick puppets are just a silhouette cut from cardboard or "fomi" and taped to a stick. Toys work as puppets, too. You can make finger puppets from large peanut shells. A paper plate, colored like a face and with elastic attached to both sides, makes a great mask. So does a circle of plastic cut from a large bottle. You can use a stick to hold the mask in front of your face if the plastic is too rigid to bend. Attach yarn for hair to make the mask look more realistic. A large rectangle of cloth can be a shawl, a skirt, a turban or a cape. Tape a paper number pad onto an old stick deodorant bottle, well washed, to make a toy mobile phone where children can practice speaking in English.

ACTIVE GAMES:

Adapt the games your students already play and make them into fun ways to learn English. Relay races, Telephone (Teléfono Descompuesto), Hot Potato and Treasure Hunts all work well as didactic games. The Mexican clapping game "Calicaturas—Presenta--Nombres de--" is fun in English, changing the words to "Looney Tunes—Presents--Names of--." Spelling Bees, Circle

Bounce (a student asks a question and bounce a ball to a classmate, who must answer) and "Find Someone Who" games are all good activities for a children's English class.

COMPETITIVE TEAM GAMES

To make a routine oral drill more fun, divide the class into teams and make a competition of the drill. If you need 2 teams, use boys versus girls, or divide the children by rows and call one half "Cruz Azul" and the other "Pumas." Shout "Goal!" whenever a child gets the right answer. During the Soccer World Cup or the Olympics, give each team the name of a country. In order to maintain order, you can count every interruption or noise as a goal for the opposite team.

You can also have competitions between the rows if children's desks are in rows (lines). Ask students to put their school supplies on their desks. Then say, "Show me your... RULER!" The first row in which all the students are holding up their rulers gets a point. When one row gets 10 points, that row wins and the game ends. This "row game" also works for prepositions. "Put your book... IN your desk!" "Put your book... UNDER your desk!"

If many of the students don't know the material yet, you can play "**Witch and Kids**." Draw a witch and 2 children on the board. Go around the room, asking questions about the new material. Every correct answer is one point for the kids, while every wrong answer is a point for the witch. Again, if the class is out of control, give the witch a point for every time a child interrupts or shouts. When every child has answered, count the points. If the kids win, draw a pot around the witch. If the witch wins, draw a pot around the kids. (This sounds very cruel, but kids love it, especially if you act the part of a witch!)

INDIVIDUAL COMPETITION

For the game "**Stop!**" all the children stand up. The teacher tells them an action verb ("Run!" "Swim!" etc.) The children have to mime the action until the teacher shouts "Stop!" Then all the children can't move. Any child who moves after the teacher says "stop" must sit down. Children who mime the wrong action also have to sit down. The last child standing wins. For new vocabulary, the teacher can model the actions, but for review the teacher can just say the words, with no modeling.

In "**Charades**," one student mimes an action in front of the class and the other students have to guess what it is, saying "Are you swimming?" etc. The student who is miming replies, "No, I'm not" or "Yes, I am." Students raise their hands and the teacher or the miming student call on the students one by one. When a student guesses the action correctly, he or she goes to the front of the class to mime another action. The teacher can give the miming students cards with words or pictures to represent, or the students can choose their own words.

"**20 Questions**" can be played about objects, places or people, depending on which vocabulary the teacher wants to review. One student standing in front of the class thinks of an object, place or person. The other students raise their hands to ask yes/no questions. "Is it bigger than a desk?" "Do apples grow there?" "Does she have long, black hair?" After 20 questions, the students have to guess the answer. The student who guesses correctly goes to the front of the room.

"Jeopardy" is similar to "20 Questions," except that the student at the front of the class gives a detailed answer and the other students have to think of the appropriate question. For example, the student at the front could say, "This state is southeast of Oaxaca, south of Veracruz and southwest of Tabasco. It is north of Guatemala and northeast of the Pacific Ocean." The other students would have to give the appropriate question: "Where is Chiapas?"

"Duck, Duck, Goose" is a circle game. The children sit in a circle. One child is "It." This child walks around the circle, touching the other children on the shoulder and saying, "Duck!" each time. Finally the child says, "Goose!" instead of "Duck!" and runs around the circle. The "goose" stands up and chases the first child around the circle. If the first child can get back and sit down in the "goose's" place, then the "goose" becomes "It," and the game starts again. You can invent variations on this game, using verbs ("sit" and "run") or different animals, vegetables, etc.

"**Touch Something... RED!**" is a game for teaching colors. The teacher tells the whole group, "Touch something... RED!" All the children run to find something red and touch it. Then the teacher tells them to touch something of a different color. This can be an energetic activity or a competitive game. If you want to make this a competitive game, tell children who don't touch something of the correct color to sit down. You could create a variation of this game, asking students to touch different articles of clothing, school supplies, body parts, etc.

In "**Simon Says**," the leader (teacher or child) tells the group to perform different actions, but they only obey when the leader begins the order with, "Simon says..." A child who performs the action when the leader does not say, "Simon says...," has to sit down. The last child standing wins.

In "**7-Up**," 7 children go to the front of the class. They are the "touchers." Their classmates have to close their eyes and put their heads down on their desks. The 7 children each touch a classmate on the head, then go back to the front of the room. The children who get touched have to keep their eyes closed and raise their hands. When all the 7 children are back at the front of the class, the teacher says, "Heads up! 7 up!" All the children open their eyes and the 7 children who got touched stand up. The teacher calls on each one of the children who were touched. They ask one of the 7 "touchers" at the front of the room, "Maria, did you touch me?" Maria says, "No, I didn't," or "Yes, I did." If the answer is yes, Maria goes and sits in the other child's place, while the child who guessed correctly goes to the front of the class and becomes one of the new 7 "touchers".

For **"Round Robin Stories"**, one child begins inventing a story. That child says just one sentence. Then the next child continues the story, adding another sentence. The game continues until each child has contributed and the story is finished. The teacher can give prompts, such as

"What did the princess look like?" or "What did the dragon do then?" Children as young as third grade can play this game if they have a list of verbs in the past and some suggestions from the teacher. For older children, this can be a fun written activity.

"Aerobics" is a vigorous activity, not a competitive game. It uses up some of children's excess energy when they are difficult to control, it focuses the group, and it helps students learn numbers. Have children repeat an exercise movement ten times while they count out loud, "1,2,3," etc. Change the movements after 10, 20, 30, 40 and so on, up to 100. The teacher can model the movements just once or do all the exercises with the children.

BOARD AND CARD GAMES:

You can make your own game boards and cards out of cardboard to play Bingo, Concentration (Memory/Memorama), Snakes and Ladders, Scrabble and card games such as "Fortune-Telling." Bingo cards could include names of letters or pictures of objects, verbs or professions. Draw the pictures, cut them from supermarket advertisements or get them from the Internet. For Concentration cards, use different colors for word cards and image cards. Cut out pictures from supermarket advertisements and glue them onto the image cards. The Mexican paper game "Basta," where players compete making lists of proper names, vegetables, fruits, countries, animals, etc. beginning with each letter of the alphabet, will be popular in English classes as well. There are many board games where students roll dice and move a piece a certain number of squares towards the goal. You can mark these squares with questions or tasks. "Pin the Tail on the Donkey" is another popular game, and teaches words like "Right," "Left," "Up," and "Down." Have students stick facial features onto a circle, representing a face, or stick body parts onto a trunk. "Twister" is a fun game for kindergarteners or smaller groups of primary school students. You can make a

"Twister" game from a large piece of cloth painted with colored circles. Make a cardboard spinner to indicate whether the player should put left hand or right, left foot or right, on a circle of each color.

(Examples of cards for a Concentration game: Question pictures.)

212

Do/Does Did	Which?	How much?
Do you like pizza? Does he smoke? Did they g	Which house is yours? Which one do you want?	How much water is there? How much does it cost?
How many?	Where?	What?
How many exams are there? How many apples do you have?	Where is Comitán? Where should I go?	What color was the shirt? What is in the box? What do you study?
When?	Who?	Whose?
When does the bus leave? When does vacation begin? When is your birthday?	Who lives there? Who is behind the curtain? Who do you talk to?	Whose phone number is it? Whose sweater is this? Whose friend is she?
How?	How long?	Why?
How are you? How do you get good grades? How is the weather?	How long is the concert? How long will you talk? How long have you been here?	Why are you doing that? Why are you crying? Why are you sad?

(Examples of cards for a Concentration game: Question words.)

TELLING STORIES IN ENGLISH IN THE ESL CLASSROOM

WHY TELL STORIES?

Listening to stories gives children practice in many areas of English: listening skills, vocabulary, grammar and structures. Stories also motivate and engage children, and work as rewards to control the group. Understanding a story in English builds learners' confidence.

PROBLEMS WITH STORY-TELLING

The most common problem that teachers encounter when they tell stories is the limited English of their students. Hearing an incomprehensible story is not fun and it does not teach English. If the teacher reads the story in a monotone, students will not understand it or like it. Some stories may also be inappropriate for the age-group. Older children prefer ghost stories or myths. They will find familiar children's stories boring. Younger children like familiar stories, and will feel frightened if they hear a ghost story or a violent myth.

MAKING ENGLISH STORIES UNDERSTANDABLE

Teachers can use the following techniques to tell stories to children with limited English or no English at all. First practice telling the story to a friend or family member who does not speak English, just using the techniques below, to make sure you can transmit the story non-verbally.

> ➢ Mime/body language
> ➢ Vocal expression
> ➢ Dramatization (alone/with students), with puppets, props, realia or toys
> ➢ Pictures/pointing
> ➢ Repetition of key words/phrases, short sentences, simple English
> ➢ Preliminary explanation of key words, using pictures, drawing, mime, translation
> ➢ Clarification, using cognates, synonyms, antonyms, hyponyms
> ➢ Questions: giving alternatives to check comprehension

AGE-APPROPRIATE STORIES

Young children like familiar stories or simple stories with a lot of repetition

Teenagers and adults prefer myths, fables, legends, urban legends or ghost stories. They also enjoy true anecdotes of unusual incidents

INCREASING INTEREST

Prepare your stories. Memorize the sequence of events and any special vocabulary or repeated phrases. Practice telling the story: reaffirm sequence, timing, delivery. Telling stories or jokes in the native language helps teachers acquire technique. Pay special attention to vocal/body expression. Give a distinctive voice to each character. Communicate your enjoyment and interest in the story.

Involve your students in the following ways:

➤ Give children pictures about story to color/complete.

➤ Ask children to draw allusive pictures.

➤ Have students repeat key phrases/dialogues with you.

➤ Ask students to act out roles: "live" or with toys/puppets.

➢ Interrupt story, or tell serially over 2-4 classes.

➢ Ask students to predict next event or interpret characters' motivation.

➢ Intersperse questions to check comprehension and increase interest. ("What would you do if you saw the wolf?")

➢ Omit ending and ask students to provide one. Alternatively, give traditional ending and ask students to change it.

➢ Have students create similar story, going around the room (Round Robin Stories). Each student adds 1 sentence. Teacher prompts students with questions.

➢ Have students choose 3 main characters: hero/heroine, helper (animal/stranger) and villain. Students imagine a problem or conflict to provide storyline, then write story/play, in groups.

➢ After telling story, give students written text for reading practice. Include comprehension questions/further work.

➢ Students tell similar stories/anecdotes.

WHERE CAN TEACHERS FIND STORIES?

If you can find storybooks in English, you'll have no problem, but it can be difficult to find children's books in English in non-English-speaking countries. A good solution is to look up stories on the Internet. Go to Google and enter: <u>Story: "The 3 Little Pigs"</u>

You will find hundreds of versions of this story listed in Google's results. The following stories are good for children: The 3 Little Pigs, Jack and the Beanstalk, Rumpelstiltskin, Stone Soup, Cinderella, The Wolf and the 7 Little Goats, The Gingerbread Man, The Little Red Hen, Little Red Riding Hood, The 3 Wishes, The Old Woman and her Pig, Snow White, The Golden Goose, The 3 Billy Goats Gruff and Goldilocks and the 3 Bears. Aesop's fables are another good collection of familiar stories for children. If you have a good story you want to tell, but you do not know the English name of the story, try using your local version of Google to find the English title. For example, in Mexico you would go to Google.com.mx and enter: Cuento: "Los 3 Cochinitos" en ingles. This will give you the title of the story, so that you can look it up in English. Collect the interesting, funny or repetitive stories and jokes that you hear, so you can tell them to your students.

Search the English Teaching Forum Online website at
http://exchanges.state.gov/englishteaching/forum-
journal.html for *"Oh, The Tales You'll Tell,"* by Kim Hughes
Wilhelm and Ted Hughes Wilhelm, published April 1999 in
English Teaching Forum Online, Volume 37, Number 2 .
The authors give teachers strategies and tips for how to
present stories in a classroom, the importance of
practicing before you present the stories, and how to
make your stories dramatic and fun for your students.

CONCLUSION

Drawings, songs, games and stories are very useful for
motivating and rewarding children and controlling the
group, as well as for teaching vocabulary, pronunciation,
structures, grammar, listening and speaking skills. Most of
the boring drills and exercises that students need can be
transformed into fun songs or games. A good repertory of
these activities is very useful.

GROUP EXERCISE:

> Do this after students find stories on the Internet and learn them.

1. The 3 Little Pigs: What material did each Little Pig use to make his house?

2. Jack and the Beanstalk: What did Jack steal the 1st time he went up the beanstalk? The 2nd time? The 3rd time?

3. The Gingerbread Man: How did the fox trick the Gingerbread Man?

4. The Wolf and the 7 Little Kids: Why did the wolf need honey? Why did he need flour?

5. Rumpelstiltskin: Why did the girl promise to give her baby to the little man? How did she find out his name?

6. The Little Red Hen: Why did the Little Red Hen finally eat all the bread herself?

7. The Old Woman and Her Pig: Why did the pig finally go over the stile?

8. Stone Soup: What did the beggar put into the stone soup?

9. The 3 Wishes: What did the man wish for first? Next? Last?

10. <u>Goldilocks:</u> Where did the bears find the girl?

11. <u>Little Red Riding Hood:</u> Why were the wolf's eyes so big?

12. <u>Snow White:</u> How did the Prince wake Snow White?

13. <u>Cinderella:</u> What happened at midnight?

14. <u>The Golden Goose:</u> Why did the princess laugh?

MICROTEACHING 4:

You will prepare a class based on a song, a game or a story. This class will be for a different age group, one you haven't focused on before. You need to memorize one song or game and one story. Keep control of the group, using the strategies we looked at in the previous section.

KIDDIE ENGLISH SONGS

---

* Recorded in UNACH Lenguas Campus III.

+ Original song by Virginia Calhoun.

+ Question Song For Delia :

http://youtu.be/eP32WXaKLt4

The Little Skunk's Hole :

http://www.youtube.com/watch?v=y62S6ZX5Aec

Happy Birthday to You :

http://www.youtube.com/watch?v=wFh-rX_Sfhs

Good Morning To You :

http://www.youtube.com/watch?v=0ltZTuOR7xY

The Alphabet Song :

http://www.youtube.com/watch?v=LtFXYvNIxws

Ten Green Spotted Frogs :

http://www.youtube.com/watch?v=SVPmtaHmL4g

This is the Way the Doctor Works :

http://www.youtube.com/watch?v=FtKIXmMnUc8

Today Is Monday :

http://youtu.be/ACFtndqofMw

and http://youtu.be/JtN7ixHO4c8

He's Got the Whole World In His Hands :

http://youtu.be/guyrERfsCB8

*+Can You Swim?

http://youtu.be/maiVHjK8UqM

Are You Sleeping? :

http://youtu.be/k8uRB3cuz2g

Finger Song :

http://youtu.be/kciPQs7KMZU

* The Ants Go Marching :

http://youtu.be/vV6gkkhR28I

Apples and Bananas :

http://www.youtube.com/watch?v=N_QybpPmGRc

* + Color Song : :http://youtu.be/qcCH2aX407E

The Eensie-Weensie Spider :

http://youtu.be/CwwUb978l_c

* Henry, My Son :

http://youtu.be/ic74ns9ln7s

Old McDonald Had a Farm :

http://youtu.be/7_mol6B9z00

Ten Little Indians ;

http://www.youtube.com/watch?v=Z_tWEayqHKk

She Waded in the Water :

http://youtu.be/ymbi8Yd1Pi8

* Oh, Do You Know The Muffin Man?

http://youtu.be/oySDnQ2CPSU

John Brown's Baby :

http://youtu.be/Pn4WtdTN4SI

Bingo : http://youtu.be/XP3SzeYGoUl

SINGING CIRCLE GAMES

* Susy is Wearing a Red Skirt :

http://youtu.be/7Xrwb2iXiMU

Head, Shoulders, Knees and Toes :

http://youtu.be/NsieDyavKMg

Bluebird, Bluebird :

http://youtu.be/mTlvPk5tBIU

Did You Ever See A Laddie? :

http://youtu.be/E88Mp1OfWXE

 London Bridge

http://www.youtube.com/watch?v=e3u6FD019_M

Hokey-Pokey

http://www.youtube.com/watch?v=UDmCSvqhhoI

CHRISTMAS CAROLS:

The Wassail Song

http://www.youtube.com/watch?v=LhkCp75LFzo

Silent Night

http://www.youtube.com/watch?v=J6P3fCDQVMI

The Little Drummer Boy

http://www.youtube.com/watch?v=7rx2g2Crjm8

We Wish You a Merry Christmas

http://www.youtube.com/watch?v=C1aguHjgd8g

Angels We Have Heard On High

http://www.youtube.com/watch?v=3-b5IC_Jsfc

The Twelve Days of Christmas

http://www.youtube.com/watch?v=M4j1paMC5SM

FINGER GAMES

Here is the church and here is the steeple

http://www.youtube.com/watch?v=ZPufWmfvEcw

Here are mother's knives and forks *(No YouTube video found)*

RHYMES AND JUMP-ROPE CHANTS

One, two, buckle my shoe

http://www.youtube.com/watch?v=d2P5bVpLO50

Two, four, six, eight, Who do we appreciate? Fulano!

http://www.youtube.com/watch?v=SdGfa_yIIKI

Solomon Grundy

http://www.youtube.com/watch?v=I1TkdTGFrGg

Cinderella dressed in yellow

http://www.youtube.com/watch?v=IwBRKdBdKuM

Pepe and Mary sitting in a tree, K-I-S-S-I-N-G

http://www.youtube.com/watch?v=8_ygLZtEHfw

BIBLIOGRAPHY

Champeau, Cheryl L. et al <u>A Taxonomy: Evaluation Reading Comprehension</u> in EFL *Forum Online Journal of English Teaching,* Volume 35, Number 2, June 1997

World Bank: <u>Developmental Stages</u>", retrieved May 2012 from: <u>http://go.worldbank.org/EWCXISU010</u>

Gable, Sara, <u>Nurturing Children's Talents</u>, retrieved May 2012 from <u>http://extension.missouri.edu/explorepdf/hesguide/humanrel/gh6127.pdf</u>

Harmer, Jeremy. <u>The Practice of English Language Teaching, 3ʳᵈ Edition,</u> Longman, 2001

Hingle, Ishbel and LInington, V. <u>English Proficiency Test: The Oral Component of a Primary School</u> *Forum Online Journal of English Teaching*, Volume 35, Number 2, June 1997

Oesterreich, Lesia<u>, M.S. Ages and Stages: Nine through Eleven Year Olds</u>, In L. Oesterreich, B. Holt, & S. Karas,

Iowa Family Child Care Handbook [Pm 1541] (pp. 202-204). Ames, IA: Iowa State University Extension.

Puhl, Carol A. Develop, Not Judge: Continuous Assessment in the ESL Classroom, *Forum Online Journal of English Teaching,* Vol 35, No. 2, April 1997

Scrivener, Jim. Learning Teaching, MacMillan Heinemann, 1994

Selby, Patrick J, M.A. Classroom Management Tips for Teachers, retrieved May 2012 from ESL Pro Systems www.esl-pro.com

Standardized Tests For Young Children? Not Yet! ACEI, On Standardized Testing: A Position Paper of the Association for Childhood Education International. *Childhood Education.* Spring, 1991. pg. 130-142.

Stevens, Gwen G and DeBord, Karen. Issues of Assessment in Testing Children Under Age Eight, *The Forum of Family and Consumer Issues*, NC State University, Volume 6, Number 2, Spring 2001

Sulich, Magdalena Keeping Discipline in the Classroom, *Forum Online Journal of English Teaching*, Volume 42, Number 3, July 2004

Testing Young Children, *Heads, Shoulders, Knees And All That* October 21, 2006, retrieved May 2012 from http://simplesongs.blogs.com/head_shoulders_knees_and _/2006/10/testing_young_c.html

Wilhelm, Kim Hughes and Wilhelm, Ted Hughes. Oh, The Tales You'll Tell, *Forum Online Journal of English Teaching*, Volume 37, Number 2, April 1999

14602492R00137

Printed in Great Britain
by Amazon.co.uk, Ltd.,
Marston Gate.